LISTENINGS

Jason Weiss

SPUYTEN DUYVIL
New York City

Acknowledgements

The author would like to thank the following publications where some of these texts first appeared: *Le Ventre et l'Oreille* (2018-2021, bilingually), "Sounds of the Body," "Bodies of Sound," "Interference," "Record Hunting," "Incomprehensible Understanding," "Whence and Whose," "Breaking Things," "Whistling Fool," "Matter Speaks," "Concertgoing 10: Senyawa," "Listening and Water"; *Interlitq* (2021), "Interviews and Obstacles," "Radio," "Listening and Truth"; *It's Psychedelic Baby* (2022-2023), "Concertgoing" texts 1-11; *Arteidolia* (2023), "Brainstreams," "Writing Liner Notes," "Prepositions"; and in the book *Steve Lacy (unfinished)*, edited by Guillaume Tarche (Nantes, France: Lenka Lente, 2021), "The Single Note."

Thanks also to the Corporation of Yaddo for a residency there, where some of this book was first written.

Special thanks to Norton Wisdom for permission to reproduce his painting on the cover.

Library of Congress Cataloging-in-Publication Data

Names: Weiss, Jason, 1955- author.
Title: Listenings / Jason Weiss.
Description: New York City : Spuyten Duyvil, 2023.
Identifiers: LCCN 2023034849 | ISBN 9781959556732 (paperback)
Subjects: LCGFT: Creative nonfiction.
Classification: LCC PS3623.E45535 L57 2023 | DDC
    818/.608--dc23/eng/20230914
LC record available at https://lccn.loc.gov/2023034849

Jason Weiss' *Listenings* is a true "Ars Auditoria" (you heard right, reader, I am making it rhyme with Ovid's "Ars Amatoria"), thus a treatise on the art of listening & simultaneously a love letter to music & all sound(ing)s. A very practical treatise based on the author's life-long involvement with this often neglected art—yes, we all "hear" but do we really know how to "listen," a very different activity? These immanentist autobiographical prose meditations concentrate not so much on what's between our ears (though that also impinges), but rather on what comes to our ears & how these—& the rest of our body/mind—can process such audio-event inputs. Indeed, we are most alive, can learn & experience most deeply if we can consciously open up to & experience the nomadic in-between of world & self, as mediated by the art of listening.

Listenings is a gathering of writings that speak not only to Weiss' life-long passion for music (& well beyond the eleven "Concertgoing" sections) but also reflect on his insights into work as interviewer ("By listening to an/other you become an/other for them; and so, together, you may understand you are the same"), as translator, as walker, as writer, as radio listener ("An invitation to not believe your eyes"), as sleeper ("The unconscious listens by its own lights, and always profits from its finds") & as everyday passenger in this world.

Trust the author of *Listenings* when he declares that "see, listen, hear" for him became "see, listen, hear, write." Indeed, as Weiss puts it, "listening is a form of travel" & that is so because "first it sends us dreaming." Listening opens up truly unknown & unsuspected areas as it gives us the "opportunity to notice a heartbeat where we never guessed."

Listen up, reader of this blurb, get this book & listen down into it. Read, I may also have said, & be all ear with your eyes, realize that "we are each a walking, talking drum sounded by wind, sun, air, others' gazes, sounding in turn through the jungle of this world."

Pierre Joris, author of *Always the Many, Never the One*

In *Cloud Therapy*, Jason Weiss described how a physical activity, swimming, transformed and opened up the way he was able to understand, and see, and hear, and feel the shards of the world that surrounds him. Through his modest first-person singular narrative, the reader was also invited to engage differently with the rest of the world through our everyday activities. In *Listenings*, he explores the more universal physical activities of hearing and listening. Whether or not these activities are voluntary or self-aware, Weiss describes and notates how they engage with and allow us to understand, and misunderstand, our own bodies, our relationship to things, to the night, to our memories, to our neighbors, to the contours of communication and miscommunication, to music, to what we understand as life. The book opens up deep levels of experience, for example, he invites us to consider whether we hear our lovers' bodies through our hands. Though listening to music is not really its prime focus, I'd swear that there's more information about understanding and living music in this book than in most of the books specifically written about music. The book is a compelling, sweet ride.

Kip Hanrahan

Contents

EARLY TRAIN

Awakening too early, well before daybreak, eyes still closed as if to imagine you might yet fall back to sleep. You try to determine what is out there. The silence folds back to reveal, what? More silence, some kind of stillness, the faintest white noise of nothing. Or is it just the world breathing, so vast it's almost imperceptible to the human ear? What is that silence, and doesn't every silence have its own nature? But then the cricks and creaks of this wooden house emerge, so infrequent they're barely noticeable. Is there a breeze outside? No clattering of the tall shrubs beneath the window. Like peering into the dark until vague forms become distinguishable, your sustained attention gathers in reports of movement, of forms not colliding but touching gently. Can you catch wind of so much gentleness? And there goes the train in the distance, long familiar, since you lived in the house as a teenager so many years ago. Did you not ever bother to look at the time when it passed? 6 a.m., say. Or did you not want it to mark a certain hour when you would rather be sleeping? You listened until it was gone. Trains have to run on schedules (except when they don't), but a train in the distance, in the dark before dawn, has always accompanied you as far back as you can remember, indispensable element of your own theater. A call, a reminder, come back, return to us.

LISTENING ENGAGEMENT

Listening is an active engagement with sounds found, sounds created. If we listen, we will hear—or we are more likely to hear. But does listening come first? Not necessarily. A sound may fall into our hearing, a voice overheard, and then we listen. Hearing can be passive or active, but listening is really an intentional, conscious act. Of course, listening can be done in a passive way, as when we turn on the radio and let it play in the background, or when we put on some music to serve as a soundtrack, a sonic wallpaper, while we do our chores or move through space. In so doing, we seek rather a mind filler, a thought dampener, or perhaps a small boost of energy through sound, whether familiar or random; it may even serve as a daydream trigger, a way to screen out the world or unquiet thoughts. Can all this still be called listening, where the medium of sound is chosen, employed, as a means of distraction? Some form of engagement remains nonetheless, for listening can also be, willingly, a subliminal act.

Hearing, by contrast, is one of our senses, something we just do, often without trying. A faculty by which to receive signals from outside ourselves, whether we notice or not. A means to be present in the world, even if that is hardly our preference. But hearing implies the possibility of understanding, as well; in English and other languages, the word sometimes stands in for both. Do you hear me? Which means, in part, do you hear *me* and not just noise. And in such a scenario, clearly, for you to hear me, you must listen.

INEQUALITY OF THE SENSES

The inequality of the senses, and of our language for speaking of them. Listen, and hear. Look, and see. Touch, and feel—already, in this last, the parallel falls apart. For one thing, touch is the sense, not feel. Taste, and? Smell, and? I had to remind myself which were the five senses, wondering for a moment if speech were a sense; in electronic terms, it has to do with our sensors, our receptors. All physically in the head, except for touch, which we think of as concentrated in the hands. Yet, as we know, our whole bodies touch. Our heads touch the sky, our feet touch the ground. Touch, taste, are senses of intimacy—though the others certainly can be as well—but these presuppose direct contact and function only at close range. Smell, the most invisible of the senses, and the most susceptible to atmospheric interference, makes a priority of intimate circumstances: food, flowers, bodily odors, let alone how those odors may or may not sketch a distinct person, along with that person's recent interactions. But we can also smell a garden, a newly tarred road, a polluted body of water, and even, miles away, a large fire. Hearing and seeing occupy the furthest range, naturally, with sight the undisputed winner: those tiny points of light that we call stars in the night sky have no equivalent for the other senses.

But our senses are also fluid, far more than we expect. They share information all the time, especially when one of them is temporarily or permanently disabled. We listen, and thus hear, our way through the dark. We see what food will, or should, taste like. We feel the rain on our skin sometimes, even in our nose, before we see it; and usually we hear it first, if it hasn't been mesmerizing us long before we knew we were hearing it.

So I recall that speech cannot be one of the senses because of its very difficulty in conveying a sense of the senses; transmuting them into word expressions, some kind of language. And to say what is felt—in the broad implication of all that is taken in by the senses—is to suppose a listener, one who seeks to understand or at least hear, or even just happens to get in the way of, to intercept, what is carried forth.

ANTIQUITY

How do we listen to early music? We may admire the attempt at authenticity, the attention to period instruments, yet we cannot erase the centuries of listening that have come down to us since. If the music sounds to us austere, can we know at all how it was heard then? In the reproduction of that antique art, how do we reproduce the listener? The enjoyment is ours now somehow, even if the music seems reduced, stripped of later possibilities, a lovely bygone relic carried down to us by the wonders of scholarship and imagination. When early music was just music, did the instruments sound strange and stiff as they do now? No doubt there were still mad ambitions and the sense that music could be all.

First Concert

The first concert I ever went to because I wanted to go was Richie Havens at Princeton. I'm guessing 1967, so I'd have been eleven unless it was at the end of the year or later. I loved his first album, and had seen him on TV—the distinctive way he barred the bass notes of his guitar, his thumb hooked over the neck, and how did his arm not fall off strumming those strings so fervently. So, I was eager to see him play live. I don't recall if the idea was my own at that age, very possibly. But it did mean that the whole family was going. If my brother was home on college vacation, it could have been his idea, or even my sister's, she was in high school. The remarkable thing is that the four or five of us went together to attend something modern, for once. A troubadour from Bed-Stuy who was a hit in Greenwich Village. More modern than Broadway musicals or the symphony.

The place was an hour from where we lived at the shore, and probably both ways driving were at night. With kids in the back. Kids who presumably instigated the excursion. I'm glad I didn't have to do the driving. All because of a 33⅓-inch vinyl record that I, or we, liked to listen to. Not that I really remember anything of the theater or the concert—was it three-quarter surround seating?—but to know that we went. Somehow that remains, lodged in a vague corner of the mental archives, even in my physical constitution. Like the memory of so many subsequent musical events.

After all, what are we left with from such experiences? A short time after, what are we left with? Occasionally a friend insists to me that they retain clearly in their mind the experience of hearing a particular opera singer or rock band live in concert, that they remember the actual music, the specific inflections of the solos, but that is not how it has ever been for me. The utterly invisible medium, made manifest in the blaze of the performance, and then the receding memory of people to convince us that we heard it; or heard something.

Of course, it may well be that I don't have it quite right, in the order of first concerts. Maybe the Monkees at Forest Hills was the summer before, not after. Jeff Kaplan's father was willing to drop a few of us off and pick us up later; or else he stayed nearby in the vicinity. An afternoon concert at the stadium, where we were too far from the stage to see very well. We could hear them play their hits, and their clever in-between banter, but wherever that vault of impressions dwells inside me, I cannot find it. Still, I'm pretty sure that was before the big concerts I went to just down the road in Asbury Park, summer of '68, right on the boardwalk at Convention Hall.

SOUNDS OF THE BODY

The sounds of your own body. Especially inside your head; sound box, calabash. Jaws chewing salad, crunching crackers, slaking thirst. Breathing almost silent not quite. Less so the more you notice. Do eyes, ears make a sound? I hope not. Tongue wagging in mouth. Knuckles cracking. Sounds down there you know where—excuse me. Maybe stomach gurgles as a cloud hangs up above.

When your body is in motion, of course, that motion lays out constellations of sound, and you can hear something of that if you pay attention. But I was wondering about the sounds of the body not in motion; sitting at a table, or simply standing up, lying down. And without vocalizing. Your body then makes little sound, outside the sound box of your head. When you are sure you can hear your heart beating, no one else can.

BODIES OF SOUND

The phrase an utter paradox. Corporeal conditions of the incorporeal. Sound the immaterial; and yet, originating from some very material body. Where we listen—a voice, a band, a grove of trees—is to hear both the sounds in the air and the entity that produced them. This notion of bodies grants coherence to the sounds. So, when we put on a record, or walk through an old house, we have some sense of what to listen for. In that respect, body becomes a very elastic concept: the wind is thus a body, so is lightning. Many bodies of sound can occupy the same space at the same time, it turns out. Our listening reconstructs them virtually. One could even undertake to compile a taxonomy; though by what criteria establish an order in the bodies of sound? Listening tells us where the bodies lie.

PATIENCE

Like all the deepest practices, listening is an exercise in patience. That is because it is not about us, so wait. Let the music, the art, the gesture unfold in the time that it takes. If a dialogue, we must respect the engagement. We listen and respond, or carry the matter further, or change course if we can. Or we listen and don't understand at first, so we keep asking questions. Time is not our enemy when we listen.

What do I mean it is not about us? Listening is to say: Here I am, I give my attention, or at least part of my attention. To all the world beyond us. Now that's a little vague, not to mention overwhelming—all the world beyond. Simply, what is outside ourselves. Other than familiar forms of music and dialogue, where our expectation is mediated by known cues, that which we listen to does not offer us a ready and measured form that could put a set term to our listening. When we stand still in the forest to take in the sounds around us, what was almost silence soon grows more and more populated. The only end to our listening is the end of our patience; the conclusion that it will just be more of the same, that we must go do something else.

Interviews and Obstacles

For three and a half decades I have sometimes made a practice of interviewing people, mostly in the arts. You might say I became a professional listener. For newspapers and magazines, later for books, it was a mode of writing in which I felt comfortable, working with the voices of others. Never made much money at it, but that wasn't the point; nor did it end up turning into a full-time occupation, except at certain moments. What qualified me for that line of work? Nothing particular, just interest. And because I said I could. Besides, when I got to Paris and realized there were a few people I would like to have occasion to meet, I wondered why in the world should they care to meet another young writer. So, I decided that writing about them might be a fair trade—assuming they wanted to bother. Generally, that worked just fine and somehow I always came prepared. But it was a special kind of listening: the questions I sketched out were like a ghost script, and I had to be ready to let go of them at any turn.

Often my questions were too wordy on the page. They just had to serve as points of departure, since from there I would follow up according to what my respondent said.

That might then trigger a question I had a page or two further in my notes. So, whatever I thought I wanted to cover in our conversation might indeed get addressed, but in a different order than what I imagined and coming from a direction I didn't anticipate. I had to listen to where the conversation was going to help it find its most natural order. If I could manage such dexterity of mind. A sort of listening ahead and behind of the listening.

Be that as it may, I also had to read the person or personality for a sense of obstacles, willingly posed or not. My very first interview, with Ferlinghetti in Paris in June 1980—to me at 24, he just seemed old and tired. Not because he was 61, about my age now, but because he knew I wanted to talk to him about poetry and jazz experiments from the late '50s in San Francisco—this was for *Jazz Magazine*—and he kept dodging me. "How do you expect me to remember all that? It was 25 years ago!" A bit less, actually. I understood that was old stuff for him and maybe he didn't remember so well, or wasn't interested and wanted to talk about something new. He had insisted from the start that the only honest transcription of an interview was with all the pauses and hesitations intact, and I agreed without hesitation. Only gradually over the following years did I understand that in fact I don't agree, because I saw how difficult such texts were to read. That principle turned out to be an illusion, in my view. When we hear or listen to an interview, we are not hearing the pauses or hesitations, for the most part. Rather, we are listening through those moments, that biding of time, we are ignoring those expressive snags in an effort to maintain the coherence of the statement. As listeners, in effect, our understanding edits out those pauses and self-corrections, except to the degree perhaps that they contribute to an overall impression of a style or rhythm.

But this notion of listening through a kind of obstacle or static applies in other settings. A year later, I interviewed the great Roger Blin, the original director of Beckett and Genet in French, amid the mess of his apartment. In what I took to be genuine humility, he asked me first why I wanted to interview *him*. Beyond that, though, I was faced with a much tougher display of resistance, or self-resistance: he had a terrible stutter. He was perfectly willing to talk about it, how that led him to acting and the kinds of roles he got. I had never met anyone who had it so bad, but I quickly learned to let him set the pace; just let him speak however he does and not jump in to move things along. And I suppose by the end of my visit I didn't much notice it.

Another early instance of this lesson in listening: a

dozen days before I saw Blin (17 April 1981), I went out to Montfort l'Amaury (changing trains at Chartres) to meet Céleste Albaret. Known to the world as Proust's "dear Céleste," she was 90 by then and some years prior had had a stroke. I'm not sure at what point during my visit I learned of the stroke; it may have been only at the end, after Céleste carefully signed my book as I requested, that her daughter told me when I was leaving. But certainly I did not know how to talk to a 90-year-old, let alone how to listen to her. That seemed ancient to me, and I could see she was slowed down. I knew she was going to have to be very patient with me, as I with her. Besides, I had really learned French just in the past year, so my ear would also be tested. With her frail voice Céleste spoke eagerly and answered my questions, happily recalling sixty or seventy years into the past like it was no problem. It helped that her daughter was there, to fill in the story and add perspective. And it also gave Céleste a chance to listen as well.

Eyes Listen

Can we listen with the eyes? Let the mind wander upon what plays before us. The road swallowed up by the car, eyes listening for what's ahead. Out my window at home, the trees in the backyard reaching—and a cat along the fence, squirrel up a branch, clouds in the sky. The window, of course, has not been washed since who can remember when. A kind of eye music springs to life. The objects around us, the traffic of things moving. So many things to look at, a symphony of happenstance. The fact is, when all faculties are in order, we look and listen in tandem, even if one or the other claims the focus. So, a primarily visual mode of attention might also be listening. At least in a shadow sense.

Concertgoing 2:
Janis, Jim, ISB

Half a century after they recorded, I listened again to Janis Joplin with Big Brother and the Holding Company, the *Cheap Thrills* sessions. I don't know how she would have lasted even to middle age, the way she used her voice. Like she was hauling a lifetime full of blues—and she was only 25! The musicians, on the other hand, sound nice but not so psychedelic as I thought I remembered, and their playing not so sophisticated either. That summer, was it 1968, I saw them play at Convention Hall on the boardwalk in Asbury Park. No, say the webs, she played there on August 23, 1969, a week after Woodstock and no longer with Big Brother. For lack of evidence to the contrary, I'll imagine that was the date. I also saw The Doors at Convention Hall, what I thought was the same summer but apparently not. Thanks to rock obsessives online, I find it was August 31, 1968, that The Doors played in Asbury Park, which poses another mystery: that was my father's birthday, just 44! Would he have let me, at the age of twelve, go off to a rock concert? Well, maybe so, all the more if my brother and sister were out that night too, maybe the three of us went together, lucky them. Recently, I found a recording on YouTube of Jim and the boys doing "Light My Fire" that very night in Asbury Park, preceded by him doing a poetry thing over some improv business from the musicians. If I saw any such art when I went, it didn't register. Sometime during the ensuing school year, eighth grade, I sang "Break on Through" and possibly that song too in a band with my friends that lasted barely a few months; we didn't get arrested. But listening to the recording of The Doors from that night, which I must have heard live (though I probably went to the early show), I am struck once more by the relative simplicity of the music, even if they do rock on for a good nine minutes. I can almost recall the excitement of going, the anticipation in advance of each song, and wondering like everyone else if Jim would behave that night.

That fall, on November 27, the eve of my birthday, unless it was the following September—these are the dates that the electronic memory bank says they played there—I went to see the Incredible String Band at Fillmore East in Manhattan. I must have been almost in heaven. I was invited by my sister's boyfriend, Joey Rubin, a guitarist in a band, who knew I liked them and offered to take me. That meant him driving the sixty miles from the Jersey shore. What did we do for parking back then? I think it was just the two of us, but in truth I don't remember the drive. No, my sister must have gone. And I'm inclined to figure it was the earlier date, since both of them were four grades older than me and seniors in high school still.

Whichever date, I only went one other time to Fillmore East and that was an escapade full of deceit, close calls, and blind luck.

My Own Voice

Funny to think that, in considerations of listening, and especially of what we listen *to* (or not), maybe the last thing that comes to mind is listening to oneself. I, like many, find it disturbing. When I recall those interviews from thirty-five years ago, I also remember the recordings—over the past few years I digitized all my old cassettes of interviews. So I thought, I could almost enjoy going to listen to those old interviews, hear their voices again, see if they are as I remember them. But then I would also have to listen to myself, hear my voice from way back when, that stumbling young man still in his early enchantment with the city. I know who he is, was, but I don't want to listen to him. Why does he sound more naked than the others? Who let him out of his cage? Just as, when digitizing some readings of similar vintage, including my own, I had to listen to the beginnings and ends for length, yet I did not want to listen to myself any longer than I had to, thank you no. Archival purposes are surely very necessary, but I have no desire to dwell on how I sound, or sounded then, and who I was or was not yet.

Smart Phone

Before the advent of the smart phone, I was unaware that it was possible *not* to hear (assuming a person's faculties were unimpaired). Not listening, fine, but to actually not hear when someone is speaking to you close by. Certain people I know can be sitting in the passenger seat, I'm driving along and I say something to them, they're immersed in their phone—as if not a sound came from me at all. Happens once, okay, but I have seen it many times from certain people I know. Always the phone, worse than a laptop or a TV: that smallest of screens, it might as well reach forth with no hands and grab the entire face firmly by the ears. "You will recognize no energy force but my own! Do you understand?!" Is resistance so futile? With tablets or TVs, when certain people I know are thereby engaged (as in always), my voice from outside in the same room may be an annoyance but heard and dispatched, chased away.

The magic face of the smart phone glows. Ignore it at your peril; leave all else behind. A voice may be speaking nearby. It is not there.

Senses in Concert

As with any sentient creature presumably, our senses work in concert. I'm thinking of our five senses, but also the uncounted ones, whatever we want to call them. Of course, they do not partake equally in every experience, and sometimes one or another may be rather absent or relegated to a minor role. But food is an area where they all have a stake. And yet, when I peel a clementine and pay attention to what I'm hearing—my eyes pleased to see the spiral of the skin separating, my fingers probing an opening between skin and fruit, my nostrils tingling at the spray of citrus, even my tastebuds anticipating that same flavor with its sudden tartness— the sound I perceive seems barely a dull accompaniment, the sloughing of a cloth garment, a mere byproduct. That leads me to consider the sounds of other dining pastimes. In a restaurant, the quiet intermittent clatter of cutlery which if it covers the conversation at the table is rather unfortunate (unless the diner is alone). A plate of pasta at home, a mix of muffled sounds. About the only food where the pleasure of what we hear matches the rest of the eating is burned toast. Our ears eagerly await the commanding crunch as we bite down.

Naturally, the other principal area where the senses most act in concert is sex. There, hardly incidental, what we hear may accentuate the allure, though the contrary can also be true, depending. Intimacy, however, raises another question: Is someone being too loud? And who is on the other side of the wall? Of all the sounds that might arise, from the bodies, from the furniture, we do not want to dwell too much on them—however delicious or distracting—lest we lose our focus.

Around Corners

At my desk, outside I hear a plane passing overhead, and that white noise hum triggers another kind of listening at the same time—that it remain like every other day, that the sound of the plane stay normal until it passes out of earshot.

So, our listening follows other sounds away from where we sit. The fire engine hurtling down the street. The telephone ringing next door, and then the telephone not ringing. The neighbor screaming at her daughter.

A cautionary listening, against big surprises. The reflex to keep an ear out. When we listen to challenging music, as it plays with expectations in unexpected ways, are we also exercising our capacity for subliminal listening, that hears around corners?

INTERFERENCE

If listening is a sort of invitation to the world, often there is an obstacle in play. Interruption, diversion, indifference; or simply a misunderstanding. We well know that the pure, unmitigated experience is out of reach or else an illusion—except when it's not—so we learn to appreciate the impurities and to take in the sound of things as they present themselves. We incorporate the obstacle, if need be, the better to hear past it.

We go to the theater, say, where a glorious symphony orchestra performs one of the crowning achievements of the classical tradition. The seats, the acoustics, everything exquisite. The music builds and builds; never did you imagine it possible to feel this close to the music, all wrapped up in it as you are. Then your tongue snags on a fennel seed stuck between your teeth and attempting to dislodge it you taste fennel again and are pleasantly surprised. Until the man seated in front of you, more dapper than you'll ever hope to be, without the slightest sign of recognition passes gas so audibly you are shocked that no one seems to notice, even as your nose confirms. But the music, the music really is sublime.

LISTENING TO PHOTOS

Choose a photograph. Once you start to dwell on what all is in that picture, think instead of all you hear there. The rustle of fabric; a fat man's wheezing; the rusty hinge on the tool shed door blowing open again. Let the sounds lift out of the photo, one by one let them emerge to deepen the fixed view. The splintered conversations; a dog yapping nearby; a passing truck roughly downshifting. Another photo, the same: the sounds that bubble forth, they'll soon fill up the room. If you were tempted to prefer silence, think again. Move on to another photo. The wind through the grasses, so peaceful; and the shriek from a bird of prey, just overhead, circling closer. You will find that it takes a lot longer to go through an album of photos when you hear what there is to hear in them.

CONCERTGOING 3:
WOODSTOCK AND BEYOND

Back in December I had celebrated my bar mitzvah, at an orthodox synagogue in Asbury Park, so by August I was ready for Woodstock. I saw the ads in *Rolling Stone*, and I managed to convince my brother to go, he was home from college, as well as my sister, she was on her way to college; he in turn invited a girl down the street and my sister's boyfriend came too, the electric guitarist; plus my mother lent her car. The lengths one goes to listen, no? What all that meant, though, besides a full car and a crowded lean-to, was the others were going to be occupied and I would mostly be on my own. No one seemed to register the slightest concern, and that was quite all right by me. How I found my way back each night very late through the vast labyrinth of people, who knows. And how our parents let us go like that, a wonder in itself.

Plenty more of the experience that I don't remember than what I do. Somewhere in the cell memory, no doubt. The first night I stayed watching concerts until 1 a.m., and the second and third nights until 3 a.m. What did I do during set changes before the next band took the stage each time? Talked with people near me; watched the peace and love circus. For three days, most of my waking hours were spent listening to live music, and I don't recall what we ate or did for food, or if we brought food and in what form. Also, no idea what I had on me in the way of money. Nor to what degree, if any, my siblings ever worried about what I got up to. How would they explain it if little brother, instigator of the adventure, got lost or went off with the wolves?

But the fact is I did not get into trouble; and I was not smoking cannabis yet or doing anything else, I would just pass the joint on to the next person. I came because there were a lot of great bands playing up on the main stage, and I aimed to go hear as many as I could. Being more on my own, I was able to engineer that. So, I did not wander too far or get distracted by side shows. Mostly I threaded my way deep among the tight irregular rows of people sitting on the ground and planted myself within a decent view of the stage. For hours and hours I stayed, until nature called or some other good reason like the rain pouring down. Which was quite a nice sound in itself, magnified by its falling on so many fleeing bodies, all making their own hurried sounds. The rain falling in sheets everywhere over the summer fields.

Funny I imagine the rain again in that setting...

After five decades of going to concerts, I can say the

mystery of live music remains intact. Memory tiptoes around in the antechamber. Glimpses of a performance may linger, impressions of tone, but from the perspective of sound, what was produced in the moment, being there is once only. Normally, a recording doesn't quite bring that back, even if it's Country Joe at Woodstock doing his modified F-I-S-H cheer. I do have one recording, though, that I made myself from the audience, which reveals a singular detail that few would recognize amid the general excitement of the music. Paris 1981, the theater at the Musée d'Art Moderne: Lester Bowie's terrific avant jazz gospel ensemble From the Root to the Source. There in the midst of the concert, when it's really heating up, you hear a gravelly resonant voice nearby calling out, "Yay, Lester!" That's my great friend Ali, right beside me. And you can still hear him like that today.

But Woodstock also spoiled me, in a way. To have had the opportunity at a young age like that to binge on so much popular music, at such a moment in its history, did that somehow accelerate my curiosity as a listener so that just a few years later I was pretty much not going to rock concerts at all anymore in favor of so much else?

Overhearing

The art of overhearing. If you're hearing somebody else's conversation, let's be frank, it is because you've been listening. Probably it started as an accident, someone seated nearby or on the other side of a wall, and then there you were, you had to know what happened. A hole in the air and you put your ear to it. We all do that, hard not to, why stop.

Indeed, wherever we go there is so much to overhear, how do we keep such sounds in their place? In the background, the above and beyond, the not-right-here. That's even less clear in a crowd, where sounds lose their place all the time. And in the age of cell phones, it's like an exhibitionist's dream with so many half-conversations brazenly on offer, practically asking us to try them on. If we are in a playful mood and well positioned, we might be inclined to listen to those partial dialogues in tandem, let our ears fold them together somehow into an almost conversation, made possible only by our hearing, our creative consciousness that makes connections where there did not seem to be any.

One of the properties of sound, as we know, is that it passes through walls and other obstacles. Miraculous creatures that we are, therefore, we can hear through walls, around corners, in recesses we were unaware of. What would an aural map look like, if we were to sketch one out? Completely subjective, no doubt, and according to a person's location. What purpose would it serve? And yet we generate such internal schema often. We know where the sounds in our vicinity are supposed to be; if the dryer, the toilet, the doorbell were heard in different directions from where we expect them—let alone if the configuration continued to change—we would be enormously confused. So, our hearing has to make sense, to some extent; likewise, we know when we are overhearing, whether or not we bother to tune in.

Mass Ear

To listen en masse to a concert, a speech, a game. Do we really hear the same thing? Is there some advantage, a side benefit, for having been even somewhat in sync for the duration of the performance? Does it do us any good, this brief communion?

No doubt the listening itself is different. If the five senses are standard equipment for the human species, the way we apply those senses is an individual matter. When the individual experience becomes subsumed in the collective, that's against the normal way of things, like a holiday from oneself. Pleasant enough for a while perhaps, but soon we may get lost. So the body brings us back to earth, each of us clunk clunk. Our own discomforts, our own distractions, these alone remind us who we are at the show.

LOTS OF RECORDS

I have a lot of records. An ill-advised modesty cautions me to clarify that I have too many records, but anyone who accumulates a substantial stock of recordings and really knows what they have will agree that there is no such thing as too many. In the sense of too much stuff generally, fine, but that's a bigger issue. The librarian in me could explain why every record on my shelves is still there after multiple purges. Rough estimate: I have maybe two thousand CDs, and four hundred LPs; most of the vinyl is shelved in the basement, bad idea but the conditions being as they are. I do not have a great sound system to go with all those riches, and in fact I listen to music these days mostly through my computer and in the car. I would love to have a room with big comfortable furniture and a great sound system, just that; likely never will. And do I still listen to all my records? One of those trick questions, but once in a while I do reach back for something I haven't heard in years. The thing is, many old recordings I listened to so much over time that they penetrated into my very synapses. Most of Eric Dolphy's records, for example. Almost as if I don't actually need to play them anymore (though I still enjoy hearing them). They're already inside me.

To this day, there is always a small stack of CDs nearby waiting to be heard. I don't listen nearly as much as I once did, and I tend to postpone the pleasure of listening to certain new acquisitions. Until I reach a moment where the thought occurs to inaugurate the disc. And so today François Tusques is playing, *Le Chant du Jubjub*, which I ordered a month ago. His performance is as playful and unpredictable as I had anticipated. A few other new releases had since ended up on top of the Tusques record, what we might call a medley of delayed pleasures, but I knew what I had and his was the jewel.

No doubt, listening strategies abound in every listener. Extended recordings I save for the car—I'm almost at the end now of nine hours of talks and performances celebrating Conlon Nancarrow's centennial, recorded in Berkeley a few years ago, imported on a flash drive. Delighted as I am to add such prizes to my personal library, it's always a question of when will I manage to enjoy them. When I drove up to Providence two months ago, for a few hours I was listening to Pablo Cueco's wonderful settings of Rabelais. A wild contrast indeed, while motoring along a modern highway.

Brainstreams

In her piece last week in the Science Times section, Natalie Angier reported how new research has at last identified specific neural pathways in the human brain that react to music. Or as she refers to that bend in the brain, the music room. Fascinated as I am to read these and other discoveries in the article, it seems to me I've been here before. The article itself was new to me, yet I felt as if I was already familiar with most of what was laid out there, not by scientific means but by my own experience as a listener. Other sounds count for nothing along the music circuits, say the researchers, and speech lights up a separate set of neural pathways. This all corresponds to my sense that we listen differently to music, words, sounds.

That music should prove as fundamental to the brain as speech, if not more so, also comes as no surprise. How could we imagine otherwise? And yet a puzzle remains, not addressed in the article: if it is so important, how can there be such a lack of sensitivity to music in so many people? Interest, curiosity, pleasure, even comfort— for some people, music stirs none of these. How is that possible? Holes in their education? Surely the condition goes deeper. Whatever accounts for that disposition, it doesn't seem right. Music is like the invisible component in the bloodstream, indispensable at a cellular level.

The distinct realms of brain circuitry sparked by music and speech confirm my own instincts in practice. At my desk, I never turn on the radio and I seldom play vocal music; the demands of language perception, from outside sources, are kept at bay. In contrast to the general sense of music as abstract, the processing of verbal meaning works the mind in ways that tend to foreground the engagement with the sound stimulus (ie. words); so, language is comparatively concrete, despite the elusiveness of its meanings. Considering sound perception from another angle, I think of the varying effort it takes to disengage from the sounds around me when riding on the subway or in some other crowded public space. Speech, nearby conversation, is the hardest to render abstract, to *not* listen to. We're suckers for anything reeking of meaning, not easy to let go of that bone. But when we are foreigners in that subway car, and the ambient conversations are in a language we don't know or at least is not our native tongue, so much easier it is to blur the meanings away. Then our thoughts can fly elsewhere while we dwell in the crowd.

Connection

Curiously, it is by listening that we feel most connected to the world. Especially to other people—our loved ones, neighbors, friends, strangers. By listening we cast a line to say you are not alone, we are here together, even across great distances.

INTERVIEWING MY PARENTS

The last interviews I did were exactly three years ago, with my parents. About seven hours recorded over the course of three days. Mostly both of them sitting there, up on the living room couch, though sometimes one went off to do something. My father was 88, my mother was 92—their hearing diminished, and my mother's voice unable to sustain long use, but they did fine. It felt like a real accomplishment to get them to sit down for that long to talk about themselves on record. I had jotted several pages of notes and questions, trying to reach back as far as they remembered about their families from before they were born. I knew it was my only chance, and even that I might have waited too long to do such a project; so, I wanted to prolong the effort as much as possible. As in any interview, while encouraging them to talk I also had to stay alert for the pacing: to cover what we could but to move things along, to corral the conversation where necessary, and above all not to tire them out too much. Since it was a solo visit, without my own family in the mix, I had seized the opportunity, but after five sessions I knew that was enough. Still, I felt a bit unsatisfied in the end, that I hadn't succeeded as well as I'd hoped. For two reasons: I discovered very little that was new to me, no big surprises (thankfully), though some lovely moments, like hearing about their meeting and courtship and early years; and, despite my efforts, we only got as far as the end of the 1960s and our move to Berkeley, barely the first half of their lives. But never mind, I am grateful for the hours that I did get.

I admit I have not yet listened to the recordings, let alone toiled to transcribe them. At the time, I had no other purpose than family documentation. I have been a little tempted to interview my mother one more time while she's still around, precisely on the theme of listening. I think it was by way of her that I first gained a sensitivity for listening, especially to music. Probably, I'll let the idea go. But how does one listen to those recordings? How do I listen to them? Transcribing is so tedious, a labor I would rather avoid, takes me too long; in comparison to my daughter who is twice as fast. So, how would she listen, how would she hear them? And whenever I do go back to the recordings, to wonder what memory writes in the margins.

Something else I understood from those interviews: how listening in that formal framework may draw a lot out, but there are stories, tellings, that will resist discovery under such lights. In those few days, due to the task we were engaged in, other tales emerged off the record by casual or causal happenstance—not, in this case, because of their delicacy, rather that was the tone of our discussions over all, putting things in place as much as one can, from a narrative perspective. But then, since these episodes didn't come up during the formal setting, or only after the recording was all done, there was nowhere to register those added threads. Inevitably, despite my listening, memory proved to be a poor stenographer.

Foreign Enchantments

The enchantments of a foreign voice speaking in a language I will never understand. In the present case, Norwegian; a new record by the harpist Ellen Bødtker with the poet Jan Erik Vold, who takes us over hill and dale, his weathered voice still full of wonder. Of course, I have no idea what he is saying except for the titles and after several times listening I still postpone reading the translations of his poems. I like hearing the voice, the actual words don't matter as much, at least not yet. His warm tones seem comforting, animated yet down to earth, telling us such stories. *Once upon a Summer* is the name of the record and also the longest piece (or rather, *Sommeren der ute*). I'm not sure I hear summer in his voice or in her harp either, but dappled moments: I just want to go where he goes.

CONCERTGOING 4:
OUTWARD

A mad plan, I would never attempt it: to account for every concert I had attended. Even if I could, what then? The music's gone; all that's left are the circumstances. Going to hear some music, and the effort to get to wherever that is supposed to happen, surely constitute an entire subgenre of narrative.

Unlike a lot of kids from Deal, I was never a Deadhead and I did not cross the country to see the Grateful Dead. But in an escapade of youthful subterfuge I did catch them at Fillmore East, in February of 1970. I was fourteen and one of seven Deal boys, we went together. We took the bus up Ocean Avenue all the way to Port Authority, sixty miles. Here too, the idea may well have been mine, but not certain. We told our parents we were going to a sleepover party at one of the boys' houses, which we did eventually, but the whole point was so we could go to the concert.

Maybe that was a bold move for a gaggle of suburban kids so young. As we filed in and out of boutiques through the East Village, we did have one incident. A bunch of local kids followed in after us and, while they made a commotion, several surrounded the youngest of us and took the cash right out of his pocket. The concert soon helped us forget all that but the next day, born socialist, I suggested to the others that we each contribute a dollar fifty so as to minimize our friend's loss of eleven dollars. None of them seemed to even consider my proposal. Was I speaking Chinese?

The Allman Brothers were the opening band, so it was clearly a memorable night, if anyone still remembers. And the Grateful Dead played on for hours, as we hoped they would. Somehow we made our way back through the sleepless city to Port Authority, got on our bus, and late in the night piled into our friend's house back in Deal. The next day, typical, I wrote a note to my parents telling them of my adventures, now that I was safe at home again.

Nothing so epic once my family moved to Berkeley that summer. I can't even recall how I got around to places for the first year and a half until I turned sixteen, driving age. Those early months, I saw the Youngbloods in an afternoon concert at Provo Park across from Berkeley High School. And in the Berkeley student union hall, at the university, I attended an unbelievable triple bill: James Cotton, Bo Diddley, Big Mama Thornton. Took buses plenty, local hitchhiking, rides when I could. But, for instance, how did I get to Pepperland over in San Rafael, noted for its quadrophonic sound system? Hot Tuna, I think, and who else. Maybe my sister drove? But didn't I go twice? Or Winterland in SF, the few times I got there (once to see the Dead). Did I engineer those expeditions too, or did I just get lucky? Not that I went out so much, but there was more on offer in my new terrain and clearly I was aware of more.

The chronology of who I saw when in those years gets jumbled up a bit, though driving age at the end of '71 would seem to mark a threshold since my mother was generous in lending me her car. Did I ever go to the Freight & Salvage in Berkeley by public transport, at its original location on San Pablo? I doubt it, kind of complicated from where I lived. I used to frequent the place a fair amount in my mid-teens, as I got more into folk and traditional music. And was I already driving when I went to Mandrake's, just a few blocks away on University below San Pablo, to hear Rahsaan Roland Kirk? In the middle of his solo, he makes his way down off the stage, and still playing strolls up the aisle past his audience and out onto University Avenue blowing his horn as if it were the most natural thing to do standing there on the sidewalk, amazing even if he wasn't blind. Who led me to that club, was it my brother? All this music I was discovering in a short span of years almost at the same time, high school tastes merging into college tastes, it was all the same town for me.

Even before driving age, in my first Berkeley years, the other poles of my listening education were the library and the radio—KPFA, with its music and literature shows. The main branch of the public library, though, right downtown off Shattuck, was my treasure house, precisely for its records. I got to borrow mind-blowing albums— the Harry Smith anthology, Unesco releases like music of the Ba-Benzélé pygmies, and Nonesuch Explorer gems like the folk fiddling duo from Sweden—and somehow I never wondered, how does all that fit into one head?

READING AS LISTENING

The written and the spoken are so intertwined that in some circumstances reading may easily be a form of listening. Correspondence from a friend. Messages and emails. Where the endless back and forth leads always to the next installment in a dialogue across many platforms. Every text that is a record of what was said, or what was going to be said. Signs of danger as well: you read the warning, you pay attention; in effect, you listen and take heed.

The reader's inner ear listens for the voice that rises from certain texts, hears its echo in the air. No one else would know it was there. I heard can translate as I read. We might not even remember which it was anymore.

The Lowly Cassette

As ethereal as listening and sound may be, there is an awful lot invested in the physical support, the material grounding of those airy transactions. In the vast chain of production technologies from recording devices to players of every sort, it is easy to forget the lowly cassette. Now, transmission is all electronic, no object needed to transport or store recorded sound, records themselves are obsolete almost (meanwhile, it's raining outside: right before my ears a reminder of the subtle tension between sound *as is* and sound that's been shaped, packaged, broadcast). The cassette was so simple and available: strange to realize that cassettes were in use for barely a couple of decades (and back once again lately), while it has been about as long since their eclipse by digital media.

I used to think of them as so many little plastic bricks, all lined up in their cases. Shelves and shelves of cassettes, I had hundreds. The 1980s were really the decade of cassettes for me. I lived in a new place, Paris; I often borrowed records from libraries and then taped what I wanted, also from friends, mostly Ali, so pretty soon I built up a nice collection of music. Early on there,

I was even taping music off the radio; plus, that was the medium for all the interviews I did too, so inevitably there was an archival angle as well—cassettes I must keep even if I never listen to them again. I still have several shoeboxes of cassettes from interviews, in the closet, all since transferred to digital. The rest of the many little bricks, with their discographical details faithfully noted on the tray cards, are stacked in the basement now, quiet on their shelves.

Only ten years ago did I stop listening to my cassettes. Because of the car. And because of the dollar van that totaled our car. No mystery here, simply that the car I bought in 2001—after more than twenty years since last owning one—had a cassette player. Suddenly, with a new used listening room on wheels, I was pulling out a lot of my old cassettes, revived from a long sleep. And I was making new tapes as well with the express purpose of—a new category—listening in the car. We usually kept a rotating selection of five or ten cassettes there, to accommodate the whole family but most of all me, the driver and chief *mélomane*. In the house, meanwhile, we reconfigured the furniture and the old tape deck was retired to an upper shelf, so the car became the last refuge for cassette listening. Then that rainy day when I came out of the gym and walking up Flatbush by the library noticed a police car with lights flashing and beyond it, a dark blue dollar van embedded in the front left side of my car, having skidded across the road at the turn out of Grand Army Plaza. When I found a new used car a few months later through my mechanic's associate, he installed a CD player, so it was goodbye cassettes. I felt like I was coming up in the world: that was the first car I'd owned with a CD player.

Next Door Chickens

They don't exactly cluck, not like I've heard chickens do in the past. And this is not a lament for the old days, when chickens still clucked the way they always did since forever. Besides, I know far better how they taste— like rabbit, of course, or frog's legs (how is it possible for an amphibian, a mammal, and a bird to taste the same?). My neighbors' three chickens, in their Brooklyn garden, make sounds unlike any I have heard (okay, not so many). A special breed? I wouldn't know. A Caribbean accent perhaps? My neighbors are not Caribbean, can't say about their charges. And I imagine chickens, or chooks in Oz lingo, sound pretty much the same whether in Africa or China, though I've never been to those two continents and recordings of the chickens there are probably not among the holdings of even our great libraries. Or is the uncommon Brooklyn chicken really special? Does clucking, or chicken talk—and can we indeed make that equation?—constitute a language? With species-wide attributes and regional variations? Clearly, chickens raise questions as well as dust. But my neighbors haven't many answers for the chickens, I think, beyond their feeding, and cleaning the coop, and gathering the eggs. In their yawp and click and whirr, I can sometimes discern a "clock clock" almost, but the chickens are steadfast, they resist our expectations. If they're telling us the sky is falling any day now, they're probably right.

Chickens don't do bird songs; even their clucking never takes flight. And Messiaen did not include them in his lovely catalogue, did he? I'm going by memory about our neighbors' chickens, for they've hardly made a sound on this bright brisk morning. Focusing on the absence of their commotion, I cannot quite make out how their sounds seem different. But then there they go again, for a minute or two, and I hear neither "cl" nor "uck," though a slew of emphatic OCKs amid an array of other alphabet-challenged enunciations. I wouldn't know, on hearing them, if they were white, but having seen them, two black and one red (or two red and one black?), I cannot distinguish which is which merely by their ruckus. I can affirm that when I first heard them some nine months ago, before seeing what my neighbors had brought home, I recognized them as chickens, albeit with some uncertainty. Not yet fully grown, rather than cheeping they sounded more like today, though less robust. Their case history, as it were, might suggest as much: one of my neighbors works at a school, which received a shipment of chicks as a project for the kids, lucky chicks; but the shipment was damaged and few survived, so the three that ended up next door were rescue chickens. They didn't look like a whole lot at first, through our fence and through their cage, but within a month they had grown to be quite substantial in size. My neighbors spent several weekends in a row constructing an elaborate all-weather chicken coop, with extended discussions as each element took shape, until at last there it was at the back taking up almost the entire width of the garden (on a block of forty or so row houses). They told me they almost broke up building the damned thing. I had remarked that with all their effort, they'll have to get more when these chickens are gone. These will be quite enough, was their response, if they last the few years expected.

In any case, the chickens are often let out of their coop to strut about freely in the garden. I have glimpsed them like that through the fence or from the back window upstairs, but I cannot tell by hearing them if they are in or out. I might guess they are more vocal when out and about, but that's just logic talking, which is no match for chickens or other creatures either. Why does our cat take no interest in them? None of the neighbors' cats seem to either. Is it because these hens are almost as big as them, with their bright feathers and strange noises? The cats may square off against each other, I hear that often enough; but never a showdown between cat and chickens (as opposed to smaller, flying birds), neither colloquy nor contest, nor even chickensian commentary.

Listening as Speech

Can listening function as a kind of speech? No doubt. And yet, on the surface, the two would seem incongruous. If we think of listening through the implication of hearing—what is taken in, often involuntarily, as part of the senses—that seems hardly to align with the idea of expression, a pushing out, utterance. At best, they appear opposite, symbiotic processes that perpetuate each other. But listening is also about choice, be it conscious or instinctive, regarding where to spend the effort amid an array of possibilities. That choice says something about who you are, how you felt that day, what you thought of the options at hand. Your musical tastes, for instance, tell us whose company you prefer to keep and even how you view the very act of listening. Further, the music you choose at a given moment, in a certain context, often conveys to anyone nearby unmistakable messages: keep out; come in; I'll show you; stay here with me. To listen is to stoke a memory—or to poke a memory—to bring it into the light of the present day, not as a ghost but as an old friend, where listening is a response to what had gone before.

And so it must be, for the present moment does not

exist in a vacuum; even the eternal present ongoing comes armed with some form of memory. In conversation, your interlocutor will not likely know who stands there beside you, summoned from the shadows, but as they speak the tone, the angle, the presence and embrace of your listening carries a hint, under the surface, of where you would go with their words. To make a semblance of listening, as when a cop or a parent seeks to lecture you, is to let them know (while not letting on) all right, we can play this game if we have to but let's not take all day, for we both have better things to do. Obviously, listening does not use words to speak, but it does use everything else: eyes, body, wind, world, even speech itself, the reception of speech. What more can listening do than to say, in effect, I hear you, I don't hear you?

THE UNHEARD

Those of us who learned to seek out challenging music at a fairly young age, how did we develop a sense of direction in our pursuits? Like many of my generation, the dissatisfactions of rock led me elsewhere, along less popular paths or of slightly more difficult access. But that is not quite right either, for I was hearing very different kinds of music at more or less the same time. When I was twelve, my college-age brother gave my mother for her birthday John Coltrane's final album, *Expression* (Coltrane had died that year). It registered with me at the time but not like Donovan or the Doors. Coltrane's music would still take me a few years to grow into.

But in the voyage that is listening to music, are there places it would be dangerous to go? No matter, we go there anyway. Even polka fanatics have their visions. Besides, it's only music, all we can do is drown a little.

I have no doubt that, more than pictures, music grants us our first glimpse of the outside: some detail that seems strange to us, that we didn't know before. The hunger for the new, the previously unheard, might be unreasonable in its way; listening for what is not there yet. Not everyone is like that, I recognize; but all listeners have their inclinations, something they want more of. Our appetite for the unfamiliar will vary with each person, as will our sense of what is familiar. However you take it, there is always an outside, a beyond, a mystery of space. Just as, if we listen to Charles Ives, for instance, there is also a mystery of the familiar. Either way, these are mystical experiences one is working toward, or at the threshold of the mystical. No surprise, therefore, that music may be intoxicating.

WRITING LINER NOTES

Any number of implications might spin out from the simple act of listening to music. Among the most ridiculous of those spinnings is the five-act comedy that unfolds whenever I set out to write liner notes. Not that I've written so many such notes—maybe a dozen times in three decades—but once I'm asked I want to say yes, and so I labor over intangibles for days, weeks on end. In that interval, most other writing—most other listening, too—gradually comes to a halt. But the brand-new record I'm writing about, or for, or on the occasion of, I listen to over and over again, and over and over some more. I listen to it every which way possible: across it, under it, in different orderings, softly, at full volume. I think, once this is done, I might not ever listen to it again.

For the longest time, though, that writing of notes is not done. How can it possibly go on for so long? I listen and listen, I scratch out some phrases, string them together, reach for the next point—and then much of it unravels. Where was I going with it? Pages of notes and phrases I'd scribbled; but find a beginning, construct a coherent text? I wish it were easier. Each day I manage to add a sentence or two, a slow accretion of reflections and statements, articulating its own sense of movement.

The music takes a while to sink in. Or rather, it takes many listenings to find a language to speak about the music. Can't be helped. I want to know as much as I can regarding the occasion for the music that I'm hearing, though may use little of that information in what I end up writing. That's the first obstacle in trying to speak of an invisible object: what to say about it. I have no interest in composing a breezy profile or tackling a track-by-track analysis; I want to say something unique to this record, so I have to find out what that is.

While I am in the midst of that writing, still listening or sometimes no music at all, it seems absolutely absurd how slow a text can be in its elaboration. This last time, I spent two weeks filling two pages. Certainly, I have considered that the slowness is all mine. And yet, trying to be coherent, to actually say something worthwhile and not waste people's time, is a matter of great pains. I do not deny that it takes me a long time each day to settle down to the task. The avoidance principle remains in play, without a doubt. Rewards are necessary too, now and then, because you know it will get done eventually, very soon it will.

On the other hand, last year, at a difficult time, I wrote liner notes in a process that was quite unlike the usual pattern. A friend, who had given me most of his records in the six years since I knew him, asked me to write something for his new record. I had imagined he probably would ask me sooner or later, though I had no idea what I could possibly say. His music is an acquired taste, and not much like anything else. I was away, dealing with family issues, when he sent me the links to the music. Before long, he grew anxious about the schedule, sooner than he initially told me, and I had neither the focus nor the time to listen to those tracks, let alone whether the very old computer at my disposal (the only internet connection) could handle it. Then one morning I woke up before six, and lying there trying not to get up yet my mind running, I began to think of the opening lines. So, I did get up and for the next hour or two wrote out the requested liner notes—without having once heard the record. I had listened to a lot of his music and seen him play on multiple occasions, in this case all of that sufficed for what I needed. I could speak more broadly about his music, and maybe it was better that I didn't have to get bogged down in all that new listening.

TREES

Listening to the trees. *Trying* to listen to the trees. Too many birds! Tiny dinosaurs with their huge whistles. Their calls, their dialogues, their conference, their orchestra; their three-note signatures. But the trees, silent as all that? I don't know the names of any of them, the birds, by their sound. Nor the trees, by theirs. Subtract the vehicles passing out on the road, lose the engines overhead somewhere in the sky. The trees are speaking quietly, taking it all in through their bark. Not the words or meanings flying about them except as qualities of voice and other resonances. The trees are listening speaking, and we hear past the wind through their hair, the lightest clicking of branches, past all those featherweights with their stubborn la di da, past the outer commotion, we listen to the trees listening, they are still here relentless in their listening.

CONCERTGOING 5:
AWAKENINGS

From 1972, when I was sixteen, through the subsequent decades, I did not go to more than half a dozen rock concerts. That was the summer I graduated early from Berkeley High School and took off hitchhiking around the country for four months with my banjo. The travels began with a ride from a friend of a friend (was it Tillie she called her Toyota sedan?) up to Weiser, Idaho, for a fiddle contest. Eventually, I went to two more folk festivals (Mariposa, Fox Hollow), and hung out with folkie types in other locales, and played my tunes for many different people along the way. Funny to think of that teenage folksinger—doctor's son, second generation, where'd the banjo come from—a few years earlier or later, not much trace of him. But while the enthusiasm lasted, I did gain a sense of music as a social community, ever expanding. And that entailed learning to listen to each other's songs, as I did at the gatherings of the San Francisco Folk Music Club, which met every other Friday night at Faith Petric's big old Victorian on Clayton Street in the Haight, where all sorts of people would come to play and listen. The American folk and blues tradition fascinated me in all its variety, the wisdom and simplicity of its forms, its lyrics, its ways of life.

All this was playing inside me like an alternate soundtrack by the time I started college the following spring. That summer, after my first term at Cal, I joined a friend to travel all over Mexico in his van and brought my banjo along; I even played a couple pieces at a *peña* in Mexico City. Back home after, maybe the same season, I went out to the Marin Folk Festival to hear a well-known group that connected something of my present with my not-so-distant past: Old and in the Way, the bluegrass band that included Jerry Garcia and Vassar Clements. But I saw a lot of people play in the Bay Area in the early '70s, and some I heard a number of times: Larry Hanks, Jim Ringer, Jane Voss, Utah Phillips, Jody Stecher, Mike Seeger (including a Berkeley after-concert house party I managed to get invited to, where he was playing mandolin, Taj Mahal on bass). At the Fresno Folk Festival, where I went with my friend and fellow folkie Patty Hall, we even managed to see an old Jesse Fuller, who played his most famous song, "San Francisco Bay Blues." But he was having problems with the mechanism of his one-man-band contraption and had to stop playing at one point. "This thing's broke down and I'm broke down too," he said. Even so, we still wanted to hear him.

Already by the fall of '73 my listening attention began drifting elsewhere, more toward jazz and other realms. I knew enough, at least, not to miss Charles Mingus when he played at the Keystone Korner in North Beach. How I learned about him, can't say, might well have been my brother, who was also likely the one to have put me onto those great 1960 Mingus recordings with Dolphy, on Candid, and his famous warning to the audience, no clinking of glasses and no ringing of the cash register either while they're playing. I had gone previously to the Keystone, to hear Bobby Hutcherson, and many times later I went—Rahsaan again, McCoy Tyner, Betty Carter, Cecil Taylor. I'm sure I felt almost grown up driving over to the city with a friend, going to a jazz club: all for the pleasure of the ears.

The ears led the way, at any rate, as I was also going out to many poetry readings in those years. My plunge into literature was propelled in part by hearing some of the voices, live and on records and radio, and even read aloud by teachers; the aural engagement was crucial, it helped give me a sense of what was possible, helped shape my own tastes. Intuitively I recognized that the most direct experience of a cultural moment was by way of the ears, how the material resonates—and how the immaterial resonates as well.

If the awakening of my listening faculties began in earnest during my late teens, the process took still other forms. That summer trip across Mexico was my first immersion in a foreign tongue: the feeling of only partial comprehension, of remaining outside no matter how hard I listen, yet finding a new passion for the history of the land, wanting to see and hear more; all that sparked a desire to study the language in college, to get comfortable with the sounds. Along another route, my early interest in politics, in the antiwar movement, and understanding the arrogance of American foreign policy, led directly to my attendance at a number of concerts rooted in folk traditions but of topical urgency: Phil Ochs, Daniel Viglietti, Inti-Illimani. For these, no surprise, I did not even have to leave Berkeley.

But naturally there was still more, and I wonder how I knew of all these things: was it word of mouth, taking cues from others' ears? There was no internet, and magazines only got you so far; none of it had to do with school either, really. I saw several spellbinding concerts, each quite different, at the former Presbyterian church on College Avenue designed by Julia Morgan a century ago—redwood interior, Craftsman style. In the mid-1970s for a while, it became the Center for World Music. I used to drive by that lovely building and then one day it was a theater. First

I ever saw Hamza El Din, the Nubian oud master with the resonant voice; his Nonesuch Explorer album was already a favorite. And there was Steve Reich's ensemble performing "Drumming," I'd never heard anything like it. There too I saw Sam Rivers's inexhaustible trio with Dave Holland and Barry Altschul, where he played a series of extended solos on tenor and soprano sax, piano, flute, the three musicians going full force for a solid hour. These concerts were like revelations to me, each in their way, in how they told me something new about music. I was just a literature student, not a musician. This was all something quite else.

RECEPTION

Messages from afar. But not too far.

Maybe all listening is a form of radio—tuning in to the airwaves—to the extent that we want to be receptive to the world.

How to boost your reception. What does that mean? Why do we cultivate sensory overload?

Would be easy to panic in listening. So very much to take in, to give its due. Who has the time?

The sense that sound information is always, at all times, echoing past us, through us, from every direction. We have but to lift our heads up to capture it.

Were the matter that simple a populace would be well informed. Let us not dwell on the resistance that instinct throws up to defend against new information. Judgment is called for, a modicum of critical analysis, discernment. A clue as to why you listen to these sounds, these voices, and not others. Because listening is reception but it is also choices, conscious or not.

The mind will wander where it will. Sometimes listening is finding the port where the mind will wander from.

TRUSTING THE DEVICES

That sinking feeling, soon after: the thought that my electronic device failed to record our conversation. The fact is, I never had any outright disasters with technology in the interviews I've done. At the start, in the early 1980s, I did have a few incidents that posed challenges. My first interview with Brion Gysin, I neglected to put new batteries in the cassette recorder, so as I sat for hours enthralled by his stories, the machine was slowing down; the last half hour ended up as high-pitched voices talking fast. Fortunately, my simple recorder had a manual speed control option. Three years later, I think it was the machine that mangled the cassette toward the end, or maybe it was the batteries again, Jean-Claude Carrière was talking about working on *The Mahabharata* with Peter Brook and whatever else he mentioned all I could gather later were the three ancient rules for theater that he invoked. But I only missed a little and that was a good ending, those rules.

I always checked the recording as soon as possible afterward, though you'd think if I was going to be heartbroken I might want to postpone it a while. For the most part, I was careful with my equipment, but I never really trusted such devices. Cassettes or later digital, it was always possible something could go wrong. Sure, given that attitude, I might have taken notes during my interviews, but that would have compromised the listening. I liked to be all ears, in the moment, for these encounters, the better to respond to any points along the way. To be busy scribbling as I listened would have been too distracting; it also might have shifted the dynamic of our conversation to that of a speech and its stenographer, a practice in dictation. So, stubborn as ever, I left myself no choice but to rely on the technology, that's what it was there for, potential difficulties be damned. Besides, these were the sort of interviews, mostly with older writers (and often not in my native tongue), that might well be published in their entirety, or so I hoped, even if their immediate purpose was for a newspaper article or else broader research. I trusted less in the accuracy of my stenography skills than in the reliability of my recorder—and I always wondered about published interviews that did not have such means at their disposal.

Indeed, it was with some unease that I regarded certain books that I had rather enjoyed, like Gustav Janouch's *Conversations with Kafka*, which I later heard referred to with some suspicion, the suggestion that parts of it were just made up. Even if not, did his notes and reminiscences jotted down in his diary produce accurate quotes of what Kafka really said? Before the era of portable tape recorders, there was no way to prove that a person actually said what they were quoted to have said. The benefit of the doubt was a lot easier to come by, perhaps. There were other such books of conversations, and clearly journalists had always been quoting people. Did the standards evolve at all, through those decades and centuries before recording devices, in what may or may not be imagined an accurate quote? However perfect someone's memory might be, or finely focused their attention on what they are hearing, there are a host of mitigating factors, starting with the most obvious: everyone's experience is by definition subjective. I am convinced that, in the realm of interviews at least, we don't always realize what we are hearing until we hear it again later, in the disembodied recording.

In any case, when I read it in college, on my own, I loved Janouch's book and underlined many passages. Decades later, I discovered Edouard Roditi's wonderful book *Dialogues*, conversations with European artists in the late 1950s to early '60s, forty years after young Gustav's visits to Kafka. I liked it so much I ordered about ten copies for friends, it was cheap on the internet. By the time of those conversations, Roditi was middle-aged and a veteran multilingual writer, interpreter, and translator. I'm sure he took meticulous notes. But still, so much of the book is presented in Q and A format; do we take that as word for word what they said (a question already complicated by the likelihood that most of his conversations took place in other languages)? And if not, what are we to expect while reading?

How, then, has the practice of listening changed in such contexts (conversations, interviews)? Did the advent of the portable recording device make us more careful listeners? More distracted too, possibly. With the mechanical advance came a certain anxiety, from trusting in the machine. But that was in exchange for the larger anxiety of recording the conversation manually; our listening no longer had to bear that responsibility. Our presence was thus reinforced. And for the new standards of accuracy in recording the dialogue we were engaged in, there was another price: more work, the microscopic labors of transcription. Listening as artifact, phrase by phrase, for reconstruction as text.

Only once did I do an interview without any recording device. That first year I was writing freelance, 1980, I went back to visit Cadaqués in September and one day I hitchhiked over the mountain to the quieter Port de la Selva. I think I'd tried to write him, but asking directions I found my way to his house, everyone in the village knew him. J. V. Foix was retired from his famous bakery in Barcelona and wasn't writing poetry anymore either; he was then 87 and had known most of the Catalan artists and poets of his time. I arrived unannounced and said I wanted to interview him for the *International Herald Tribune.* He let me in, but when I started to take out my cassette recorder, he said no machine. I hadn't read very much of him, just in anthologies, but I had liked his spirit and knew he was important. I didn't imagine a long interview, I didn't know enough, I was only 24. So, we talked a while in Spanish, I listened to him, maybe scrawled a few notes. When I took my leave, I walked down to the first café, and sat at a table. I wasn't going to have room for a lot of quotes, plenty of background would be needed for an English-speaking readership that knew nothing of him. I proceeded to write down everything I could recall hearing not one hour ago. I saw I might be able to manage without a recorder if I really had to, but why would I ever want to do that?

Record Hunting

What are we searching for so assiduously? To hunt, dig, excavate; unearth from the vaults.

Recorded music is far more complicated than meets the eye. Visually, it's as if nothing, a wafer, a ribbon. But what is embedded there in that nothing can reach astronomical value or promise the most arcane of illuminations upon listening. Or, it is just one more record, like a billion others.

We don't know, and because of that we spread out through the record stores and flea markets and library sales, our fingers walking the stacks, ever on the trail of a find. How will we recognize it when we see one? The aim is not simply to add another item to the collection, or to snag a few bargains, all very nice but we're a little beyond that. We, the tribe of discerning listeners, must keep looking. There are always records we didn't know about, that may or may not be worth having, no need to be a completist. The mental cataloguing also has to be fed, as much as the ears. Sometimes it's enough to just read the cover and imagine the rest.

Still, I wonder what will jump out at me, each time I step into the alternate universe and extreme sport known as the WFMU Record Fair, as I did the other day. What recording will suddenly land in my hands that says do not let it go? I dodge the vinyl completely, mountains and mazes of vinyl the past several years, though I may take a glance the next time. I don't care about the stamp collecting aspects, the rare pressings and alternate album covers, it's only the music that matters and some old albums never made it to digital. Instead, I comb through the CD stacks, especially the many $3 bins, while a whole elaborate inner dialogue plays out with each title I linger over. Faint sympathetic tones echo from across five decades of listening to recorded music, as I whittle down the reasons for keeping all but a few of my selections. It's amusing enough to see what resonances are struck in the mind at the mere sight of a name or a cover, and like a keyboard full of Proust's madeleines, an internal sampling reflex, my thoughts bounce around an entire lifetime, and further. A couple of years ago at the record fair, deep in the $1 stacks which I normally consider a waste of time, I chanced upon a CD by Kolinda, which turned out to be (as I'd suspected) the Hungarian folk group I heard on record all the way back in 1980, when I was living in that crumbly neighborhood in lower Montparnasse, on the Rue du Texel near Pernety—a neighbor on the ground floor played it for me and let me make a cassette copy, which I still have in my basement, Bernard committed suicide not long after I moved across town, I could still recall the tonalities of the group's sound, and so for one dollar I had a later record of Kolinda some three and a half decades after first hearing them. Clearly, when we listen to a recording, we are listening to so much more.

Something else about the $3 bins at the record fair: a reminder how popular artists live on. I saw live recordings by the Doors and Jimi Hendrix that I'd never seen before (not that I've kept up), probably released in the last decade or two but nonetheless many years after their deaths. I resisted the urge to feel like I had to buy them. Even in the sixties—half a century ago—an awful lot was recorded, so we never know when a new record may yet come out of someone long gone. Indeed, we like to be surprised by such discoveries, as if to remind us that time may be circular or built on resonances as much as linear, and that we might still hope to hear from the lost.

Whether in used record palaces like Amoeba in California, or the WFMU Record Fair, I think that is what drives our perennial search. The thought, for me, of a previously unknown recording of Chris McGregor surfacing, or further back, Herbie Nichols sessions. Records that don't exist, that might have at a moment unaccounted for, that suddenly materialize almost because we went looking for them.

FIRE

Breath. A breath. Breaths. Breathing. Listen to your breathing.

But when I read the news lately I am reminded of the opposite of breathing—*fire*—and I wonder how that sounds. I think I might know, but really I have no idea; I haven't witnessed more than a campfire. Movies and TV give us plenty of conflagrations, but also talking horses and time travel, so who knows. The massive fire raging out of control up in Alberta, Canada these past weeks, leveling much of the oil sands boomtown Fort McMurray, has me trying to imagine sounds no one will be able to hear directly. No mention of casualties; eighty thousand people evacuating. I suppose by now someone has built a completely fireproof multidirectional microphone that could record or transmit the sonic drama of the fire's advance. A few such microphones could be left in key locations before evacuating and operated remotely. The record of a ghost coming through, devouring everything in its path. The snap of the air as breath is sucked out of it, the husk of the heaving wind. Vast wooden structures liquefying in collapse.

Sound artists get up to all sorts of incredible, quixotic

ideas: probably more than one is already working with the sounds of fire. But is there an ethical dilemma in seeking to capture that byproduct of a destructive natural force? If the artist or investigator hasn't set the fire, and no suffering was the cost, then sure have at it, let the fire speak and moan, threaten and cajole, let it whisper and bellow in its thousand unimagined tongues. Playing with fire, even as sound material, may invite warnings and disclaimers. Regardless, the fundamental question is how to treat such material. How to render it and not just make it an effect? Dare we try to work with those sounds? And to make what?

As a listener dreaming up these scenarios, I still wonder about hearing the great northern fire from inside. Yet only as sound, what does it mean to us without the sight of the flames? Can we still be mesmerized or sent into a panic? Do we hear anything more than something is burning? We might not be able to stand it for long, no matter how composed. Or it could be, after all that effort to harvest those sounds, we don't recognize them in the slightest. Neither our breath nor the fire's breath.

GAP TOOTH WHISTLE

A friend tells me of attending a gala benefit the other night, and being seated at a table right next to the stage, so that when it came time for speakers and performers she was sitting very close to them. Someone important gave a short speech in introducing the guest of honor, but he was missing a front tooth and all she got, my friend, was the sound of the whistling that caused rather than anything he said.

Easy to imagine listening and the wispy sound of that whistle rising into prominence and receding again like a loose flap, ever sibilant, thus diverting the focus of the listening. As in a movie it takes over, rending the gentleman's words like so much confetti.

Afterlife

Memory has its proclivities, almost independent of the one who remembers; how, though, does it manage to skirt the real, the concrete, the physical busyness of a body in time, in favor of sense impressions, experience spun from the afterlife of light and sound?

INTERLINGUAL TRANSCRIPTION

Most of the literary interviews I did in the 1980s in Paris were done in French. But since my thoughts were toward publication in English, a curious process developed. When I transcribed the interviews, listening to the French, I wrote directly in English. Though the recordings still exist, there is no transcript of what was actually said, only a translated transcript. Or rather, a transcript that is a translation of what was said. For my purposes at the time, that interlingual listening was the most efficient way to handle a time-intensive task. I felt, too, that hearing the writer speak would help make a more faithful translation. And in the meticulous listening that is the act of transcribing, I found more than a few French lessons. My ear at the level of individual breaths, language laid out like a brick road. To write what I hear but as if seated in an interstitial place, at a flip in the language switch. Metaphors can't get at what's going on really, too complicated. But that expediency is all around us, where the original text does not exist. We make do with what we have, and the fictions build from there.

Think if we got it wrong somewhere in the translation. We didn't hear what we thought we heard. The wind got in the way, noises. It would not be the first time that a history, a culture, grew out of false assumptions. And we were listening so carefully! Did our distraction take the language for a spin? Or did we just not know it as well as we imagined? Interlingual listening presupposes, after all, a certain fluency in the sounds of the language heard; we become interpreters but to the page. The more I think about it, how could there not be cause for worry? When I listen in my own language, I get things wrong sometimes. So, it's all the more likely when transcribing from another tongue, no matter how many times I listened to some parts, that I got details wrong now and then. Of course, I don't think I did. But I'm not going to know.

RADIO

Broadcast radio must have started as a proto-surrealist invention, an elaborate gag that got out of hand. Open a drawer or a door and out come voices, music, a comedy at your expense. A box of the disembodied. An invitation to not believe your eyes. A turn of the century reduced to the merest twisting of a knob.

It's funny how a device made for mass enjoyment can feel so personal. For more than fifty years I have been listening to radio. Especially in my teenage years and my twenties, I learned a lot there. I suppose I must have been alone most of the time I was listening—isn't that when we are most receptive, even most impressionable, when we're alone, all the more so in our youth? Sent forth from some mysterious corner, a slight tickle of soundwaves seeps into our wandering mind, emanations from a holy ghost yearning to seduce; or simply because the ghost as well is alone. When we are with others listening, it's just a broadcast in the background, pleasant enough, a shared experience that nobody has to think about much. But taking it in on our own, with no one to keep us from the temptation, the music or talk might well transport us. Such was the illusion of the radio voice that by the simple act of listening it seemed almost as if that person were talking right to me. The radio itself, that box of wires and transistors, was just a receiver, of course, and I, in choosing the station, was the receiver of the receiver.

So, what was I doing during those moments? In the past decade and a half, I have only listened to the radio when driving the car, but as a kid, a student, a young dreamer in my room, how was the body occupied (or not) while the ears were thus engaged? I can almost hear Erik Bauersfeld again on KPFA reading Kenneth Patchen at the beginning of the seventies, or a couple years earlier the velvety voice of Rosko conjuring mystical gardens from Kahlil Gibran on WNEW, yet I cannot see any occupation but the listening. Maybe homework, reading magazines (early *Rolling Stone*, Brautigan era), talking on the phone—or who knows maybe just sitting there listening, looking out the window at the trees possibly, even writing something. As if to wonder whether listening to radio was only ever a distraction, or did something linger, even sink in perhaps, some kind of spirit? Programming, voices, productions of endless sorts; voices talking to us, carrying us over to somewhere else.

INSECT EARS

When I hear the tiny, high-pitch buzz or catch sight of a small insect or mosquito hovering by my nose and I clap my hands—in the likelihood that I miss, is the creature sensitive enough to feel the waves of that loud clapping?

CONCERTGOING 6:
AVANT-GARDE

From the time I was eighteen, nineteen, I began to get up to date on the jazz avant-garde. That meant a lot of listening, buying records as I could—Braxton, Lacy, Art Ensemble, also earlier innovators—plus borrowing records, finding radio shows on KPFA. Getting to go see that kind of music played live was more difficult, likely because I just didn't know it was happening or else there really were not many places to hear it in the Bay Area. Somewhere in there, I managed to catch Cecil Taylor in concert at the Keystone, with Jimmy Lyons and Andrew Cyrille in the band, who all showed a remarkable instinct for keeping pace with each other at such an intense level. I also saw a memorably disappointing set of Pharoah Sanders at an odd club on Telegraph corner of Haste, a building that for the past couple decades has been the Berkeley outpost of Amoeba Music, the used and new records wonderland, but back then had a new age juice bar slant, rather forlorn with all that unused space. Pharoah himself played well, his big raw tenor sound reliable as ever, but his presence onstage and his direction of the band, such as it was, became a prime example in my mind of how not to play a set. I mean, if the audience matters. With each piece, the routine was exactly the same: he played the theme, which led into an expansive solo, and when he'd had enough he walked offstage, sometimes to the back of where the audience sat, while the band proceeded to wear out the piece with the same order of lackluster solos every time, until Pharoah came back onstage to close the tune. On the other hand, possibly the first I heard of the new crop of jazz adventurers playing live was an Anthony Braxton concert in '75 or so. How I learned about it, beats me, a notice in print or mention on the radio; only now, glancing around the internet, do I realize he passed through the Bay Area several times in those years, though somehow this was the sole occasion I was aware of. Seldom a regular reader of the jazz press, I did pick up an occasional issue of *Coda Magazine* from Toronto and was by then a subscriber to local writer Henry Kuntz's newsletter *Bells*, an invaluable guide for me at that moment to records and improvisers I had yet to discover. I also had several of Braxton's records from the previous half-dozen years: the double-disc solo on Delmark, *For Alto*; two records from BYG with his great Paris quartet (my introduction to Leroy Jenkins, Leo Smith, and Steve McCall, as well as to the AACM in general); and his first Arista releases, reflected in the concert we were attending.

So, my brother and I and a friend drove the fifty miles down to San Jose State and Braxton presented an exciting concert with several ensembles: a sax quartet and a large group featuring some of the best young improvisers from Chicago and Saint Louis (including Roscoe Mitchell, Julius Hemphill, George Lewis, if memory serves), and also duos or trios with Richard Teitelbaum on synthesizers. For a first dose of all these musicians, it was quite a night.

The idea of a listener's history: is that not both impossible and pointless, without importance? And yet, we went to so much effort to hear what we did, to listen to that music unfolding. As if it were part of our education, part of the air we breathe. We want to remember whom we have loved, and so music is also like that. Cherished companions, fellow travelers.

In those years I was a college student, I lived at home, poetry and literature were my main engagements, and by 1976 still in my junior year I had a steady girlfriend. All to say, the forces calling my attention were numerous. Added to that, as a writer and a poet I became very interested in theater, I or we went to a lot of plays. In every direction I was tuned in to words and speech, and so the pursuit of music, ever constant, was like a secret channel, a reflection of pure personal curiosity and pleasure.

After listening more and more to the younger improvisers, somehow early in 1977 I found out about an incredible series of solo concerts through the winter and into spring, at a small club in south Berkeley on Adeline Street called Mapenzi. Many a reference to that series I have seen in the forty years since, and glancing at the roster now I'm surprised I didn't try harder to catch every concert. It was a very significant series, as the small audience knew at the time. I didn't keep a record of who I saw, but I vaguely recall that I went to hear solo evenings of Oliver Lake, Leroy Jenkins, Don Moye, maybe Joseph Jarman, Leo Smith. Any chance I saw Julius Hemphill there? I don't think so, but I wish. As if that concert still remains inside me and the right spring could bring it forth, assuming I went. There were others in the series too, and it's incredible how such a high caliber of musicians came through the Bay Area in an ongoing way like that for months. Did Mapenzi produce it all, cover travel and lodging for these musicians who each played two or three nights? The club seemed too small for that, less than thirty seats I think (forty years later, I'm still going to hear music in places that size). The interior was marvelous, a lot of sculptural and assemblage aspects to the walls, African inspired, to the tables as well, very beautiful, the eye always had interesting corners to alight on. That the music was being heard in such a special setting was not lost on us.

In thinking back on some of the concerts I've attended, why do I often recall the venues more clearly than the music played there? One obvious reason is that the physical space, especially sitting inside that space, not to mention the route taken to get there, sets off a complex weave of spatial perceptions and internal mapping all on the way to experiencing the acoustical events, whose physical dimensions remain invisible. Though I have surely gone to far more concerts on my own than with friends, it might seem the social occasions would offer more for the memory to hold onto, but I cannot say that is the case for me. However, as with certain record labels that develop an identity by the roster of artists they cultivate, frequenting a place for its programming or just a single series of concerts locates it in the mind as somewhere familiar, a particular place and time where a kind of family of sounds once lived.

There was one other concert series that was important to me before I left California for good at the end of the '70s. After a first visit to Europe with that Berkeley girlfriend, in the summer of '78, I moved to LA to study screenwriting for a while at USC. I only lasted a year, thinking often of Europe, but someone gave me the name of Lee Kaplan or maybe I met him at Rhino Records. Musician and book guy, he produced a series of new music concerts at the Century City Playhouse that year where I got to see some of the finest improvisers in LA: Bobby Bradford and John Carter, Vinny Golia, Horace Tapscott (didn't I go hear his Pan-Afrikan Peoples Arkestra in South Central after that? or did I just wish so?), Buell Neidlinger and Marty Krystall's band, Glenn Ferris (whom I was surprised to see again the following year, sitting in with Lacy's quintet at the Dreher in Paris), probably Nels Cline as well. Again, what an amazing series to have seen, and all those musicians lived in the area. For me to behold such ears in LA—where I did not take naturally to the lures of Hollywood and I was still quite young—was to find reaffirmation of the creative life, whatever that turned out to be.

THE INSOMNIA WRESTLER

He wrestles with the insomnia of those who come to him, who arrive bleary-eyed imploring him to do something. They talk and he listens. He talks and they listen. They come back next week, he listens and wrestles. It isn't easy at all. He wrestles what they cannot see. Listening to them is not easy, watching them get in the way of themselves. He helps these people apprehend their ghosts, to be locked away in a dungeon; or in a golden cage, on a proscenium stage.

His insomniasts will talk and talk and talk, given the slightest opening. Have they no off-switch? Probably they would bore a hole in his listening if they could; fill it with their demons. He remains so calm somehow, retains his sense of humor. Is he listening to the wind in their words, the waves crashing on the rocks of their heads? Does he hear through to the great silence, the quiet mind they seek? What they wouldn't do for a good night's rest.

Insomniasts are relentless, desperate, perversely resourceful in their endless somersaults off the absent springboard of sleep. Does no one else hear their muffled agony? No one beside them at night, or at work or at play, knows how to listen to them or even to see they are not there. But by the sound of their voice, he recognizes them speaking from their lost wilderness and can guide them to safe harbor.

How do they not tear him along with them, engaged as he is (for a little while) in their struggle? How do they not infect him with the residue of their stubborn absences? When he goes home at night, weary from battle, from the blinding bats of all their talk talk talking, to listen to nothing but the old familiar music, how does he not fall through the tenuous fabric of his life? He might call out if he did, like someone suddenly drowning in the midst of a teeming crowd, only who would listen?

SHOWER DRIP

Water drip. Drop. Drip. When you've lived in California, if you're conscious, you learn to not take water for granted. Some forty-five years ago, after my family moved to the West Coast and the concepts of ecology and recycling and drought began to filter into my teenage mind, I took on the habit of turning off the shower between first getting wet and later rinsing off. Beyond the pasty sounds of wet soap and its lather applied all over my body, a sampler of the house noises emerged as if in an unguarded moment, an interval in which the soundbox of my head was not immersed in that rain pouring down upon it. A toilet flushing through the pipes; warm air rattling up along the central heating ducts. Out the bathroom window, the trickle of the little stream below, the *haa-haa-haa* of the whateverbird, the thin descending whistle of someotherbird. The sounds around me surfaced unbidden, until they washed away again.

But enough of my shower habits. Except to note that a certain small instinct took hold as well, a reflex of the ear, alert for the signatures of waste. I am often surprised by what others do not seem to hear. The toilet running: which thus suggests that anyone who so left it should bother to get up and jiggle the handle (unless that task falls to the person who couldn't help noticing the problem). What gets me the most, though, is the dribble drip drip in the men's showers at the gym. One stall in particular, and others too sometimes. I don't know how, in a place where people go to maintain or build their strength, so many can be so oblivious that they do not bother to shut off the faucet completely. How can people be so careless that they manage not to even notice? I listen without trying for the drip drip drip, and if I'm merely passing by the showers on the way upstairs to the machines and the weights, I'll make a detour to turn it off. And certainly, if I'm in a stall nearby, amazed as I am to see the person walk away (even someone I know) and leave the dribbling behind, I wait till they turn the corner before I step over quietly and shut the handle.

FATHER'S MESSAGE

"**W**e are *not* available! Please leave your telephone number and we will call you back!"

In the manner of a stern warning, the words carefully launched onto the message machine, my father's voice still endures a year after his death. I call my mother's number just to listen to it again.

Did he mean to tell us rather, "Stay away"? Or was that tone of his more like, "Leave a message if you like, for all the good it'll do you, I won't hear it anyway"? Like many old people, he was hard of hearing in his last years and refused a hearing aid, but even if he didn't want to hear, we just spoke louder, so he had to listen. For all the good it did us, or him.

My mother never hears that message. Why would she call her own number? She doesn't need to listen to that voice to know it's there—or rather the recording, since she makes no pretense otherwise. But to those of us who call, family or strangers, and land upon his message, we are confronted with a mystery: not so much the voice beyond the grave—in its simple fact a conundrum, sure, with its straddling of dimensions, though hardly a rare occurrence in the modern age—as the specific gesture of this voice that we chance to hear. Like any recording, it is the stamp of a personality printed, marked down, engraved, at a particular moment in time, before which only our listening changes. The purpose of the message is supposed to be one of reception; yet, hearing it, such an intention seems far from certain.

ACCENTS

I don't speak English with an accent. I listen to myself speak: absolutely no accent. You can't tell where I'm from. I mean, you can hear that I'm American, and not from the South, or Boston, or the Bronx, but beyond that, who knows. That's because I do not have an accent. When I listen to many people, right away I can tell they're not from here. Well, I'm not either, from here, this city. And I know people who were born here, lived here their whole life—some of them, their accents, classic; while others, not much of anything. I don't know what it is, if there's a neutral, generic American manner of speech, that's probably how I speak.

The prevalent Anglophilia among educated Americans begins with the accent. But to cash in on that accent in America, one has to actually be (or seem to be) British. How cute, how funny, how hopelessly sophisticated. No doubt there is also value added in speaking a French- or even a German-inflected English, though surely that's a smaller set of Americans to be so impressed. This dynamic of expectations on hearing certain accents has a unique character among Americans, I think, at least among those of European descent, as if hearing the old country speak again demanded a special reverence, and even a weird nostalgia.

Despite all my listenings, none of that European thing ever worked much on me, perhaps because I didn't hear it in a way that touched me directly; and too, because I started out as an Americanist, north and south, before I looked at Europe. To this day, neither a Londoner nor a Parisian can I recognize by their accent, and yet I have long been able to detect a *porteño* accent whenever I hear it on the street, in Brooklyn or elsewhere. I've talked with a lot of *porteños* over the years, some were close friends; all contributed to a sort of sound portrait in my mind of life in Buenos Aires. It got to the point where I was even speaking with *porteño* pronunciations for a while, under their influence—just as, in my initial years of speaking the language, in California, I was hearing more Mexican Spanish.

But one thing I can assure you about the way I speak my native tongue: whatever you want to call it, I do not speak with an accent.

PREPOSITIONS

One of those words that bear an implicit assumption of a second word, usually a preposition. Listening *to*. What? That is the most immediate dynamic adhering to the single word: listening—to something.

Fine. We could be at it for years just on that, drawing it out. But we might also consider other prepositions, to start with. What do they do? What nuances do they awaken?

Listening at. The limits. The speed of. An altitude of. Listening after. Dark. Making love. Listening into. The deepest corners. Your heart. Listening behind. Your movements. Walls. Listening from. A quiet place. Fear. Up a tree. Listening past. The graves. The noise. Listening on. A whim. A mountainside. Your Aunt Betty's rooftop. Listening through. The lousy melody. The stuttering. The water. Listening under. The house. Your breath.

Most often, there is still the sense of *to* lurking. But what about just listening, without any prepositions. Is listening lonely? Does listening not know what to do by itself? Listening is a form of attention. It happens both voluntarily and involuntarily. She was not trying to listen in on our conversation. Do we not listen, frequently enough, without our full attention? Our willful attention will likely be marshaled when we listen *to* something, but there is also a kind of listening that pulls in everything out there, open to the full spatial complexity of a given place and time. Listening indeterminately, yet in appreciation of what is found.

Are these modes of listening, these shifts of inner mechanisms and balances, mutually exclusive? Our listening can do it all, if we so choose. You can hear the lovely music along with the movements of the crowd and the wind through the trees. No need to be distracted. You are part of the concert.

NEIGHBORS

Last week, from a house or two beyond next door, an enticing sequence of jazz recordings from the forties or fifties drifted over the back fences. Names and dates eluded me, but I had long been fond of the style. Interesting choices, I thought, who is this newish neighbor? The various pieces sketched a kind of portrait, however fleeting (I hadn't yet considered that the playlist might have been curated by some algorithm): a person of substance and discerning taste, no doubt. I wouldn't want to give them too much credit just for a few tunes, but it might be worth meeting my neighbor, see where they come in to such affinities. On the other hand, that music cast through the air was not exactly sharing, was it, nor an invitation. What could I really determine about this person? Should I respond with records of my own? And to what end?

Another day from the same direction, the voice of a father playing catch with his little kid. Making a big show of it to entertain his child or himself, the kind of overblown parenting that leaves me cold. Does his unimaginative routine tell more about him than the instant personality of some records, if they were his? Cool and corny don't seem to mix, but maybe, how to reconcile. This afternoon, coming from directly in back, I think, one of the houses facing onto the next street, musette music (a disc I might have) followed by a gypsy jazz version of "Lover Man" and then more musette accordion. Who are they? Is that indeed a different house? My imaginary portraits were wobbling. Out my window, I cannot see much of the neighbors, and the little I can doesn't add to the picture. And are the musette people the same where a girl practices violin now and then? She has gotten better, playing all sorts of things—"Theme from Mission: Impossible," the old fiddle tune "Cripple Creek," a creole cotillion.

I have sometimes wondered what image of myself I was throwing out into the world when playing music loud enough for others to hear. Does a similar thought occur to my neighbors at all? The phantom presence of someone close by, within shouting distance. You don't know who is there except for the music which is almost becoming familiar.

WHITE NOISE

Sound as screen. In summer, the constant electric fans going full force, air conditioners chilling. To each its diffuse hum, its access of oblivion. As if we might hide behind that noise without features or form, without directionality, steady, unvarying, full of nothing. Cast off by so many motors and machines, like a thicket of sonic dust, it would flatten us—except somehow we manage to ignore it, to make of that mash the merest background. And let us not overlook its screening properties, which do prove useful. When I first knew my wife, she had a white noise-making machine, I wondered if that was a New York thing: she turned it on at night against her landlord's son who lived in the apartment below, with his parrot and no insulation in his ceiling.

But why white, the noise? For its dullness? Or else like the snow when one goes snowblind? Because it can swallow up all other sounds, like white all colors? It would stop thought in its tracks, heaving a kind of aural cotton or cushion between everything.

In the natural world, there is no white noise. The rush of water, or wind, for a moment perhaps, but then that changes, again and again. White noise is absolute sameness forevermore, and only manmade.

LISTENING AND TRUTH

A curious dynamic arises between listening and what I will call truth. Most sounds engage no great complexity in that regard, they are what they are. Like them or not, we take them in because that is the world we find before us. Urban dwellers know that most of the sounds around us are human-produced, and many of these are like waste products: motor vehicle noises, construction, airplanes. If we listen at all, it is for the few threads of information they convey in the background. Where barking dogs and bouts of bird talk reside as well. But when human expression enters the arena, there the ambiguity sets in.

To this day, I have always wanted to believe people when they tell me something. More than their emotional truth at that moment, I expect the matter to be just as they say. That I often know better seems a measure of my disappointment. And yet, I am easily fooled in the first moments, since my inclination is to take words at face value, rather than wonder what they really mean or who is speaking them. So, here we also have the question of trust mixed in. Implicitly we make distinctions: my friends I trust completely, and even most people I might meet I would tend to trust, carefully perhaps, until suspicions grow. When I listen to public figures, however, trust becomes an image issue, and I know that any truth in what is said is for public consumption—it has to sound good to someone, whether it's true or not. But even with friends, we have an instinct to listen critically on some level, to know all we can from those words. How, then, do so many people suspend their disbelief so completely, as in the current moment in America, when listening to the rantings of a tawdry and pathetic personality? All right, those are my words; for such people, the candidate appears to be their savior. But still, I find it incredible: how does one manage to *not* listen critically?

Listening to anyone speak—*if* we're listening—by engaging us in language, launches us in the perilous pursuit of a kind of truth. We may not choose to recognize our part in the contract, as it were, but such is our responsibility as social animals; as listeners. That does not require us to act as inquisitors, or judges, or policemen either, simply to try to understand what is being said. The same words spoken by another person, or to someone else, may carry quite a different meaning. If we sleep through it, we might not get another chance to find out.

Though ambiguity may stalk human expression—we do not even know our own meanings entirely—the realms of art can salvage inherent uncertainties and turn them to advantage. Ambiguity proposes potential richness, greater resonance, if the vibrating tensions are left to sound off of each other. So in language, in literature. For music and visual art, mostly unburdened by the gravitational force of meaning that words carry, we seek a coherence on its own terms, complexities and all. But how do we listen for truth in music? Will we know to recognize it? Or is that only the domain of words, at best?

EAR UNBOUND

Where the human ear cannot go. Certain sounds, and certain perspectives on the sound environment, can only be reached through technology. Mikes are placed, and the documentarian withdraws. Thus, if captured, then composed. Study and commentary; study and departures. On the level of insects in a moor and their mating calls, or vultures tearing into a carcass—as today's *New York Times* describes the work of field recordist Chris Watson, in an article on sound hunters. The opportunity to notice a heartbeat where we never guessed.

It may well be there's an element of exoticism in seeking out such sound experiences that we would not ordinarily know. A challenge, a sort of forbidden fruit, or plain old curiosity about all that exists beyond us. We will never come to an end of the dreaming, somehow there is always more. Soon as we de-center the human presence— as if there were any way we could listen *not* as humans— the realm of the familiar opens its vast storehouses. At the same time, as seekers of sounds, we do not want to be limited by our own bodies in what we can hear. So, tools are devised, and the most clever methods, for listening to the world from other angles. But time remains inviolable:

unless it was already set down, we have no way to listen across time to another moment; when that moment was (or will be) the present. The recordings only capture what can be recorded.

Another focus of the sound hunters article is Ian Rawes, who created the London Sound Survey website which makes available a voluminous catalogue of field recordings he has made all over the city; not hidden or hard to reach sounds, but rather sounds right in front of him. A project worthy of Borges or of the Académie Française with their endless dictionary, never to be complete. Aware of his project's historical importance, he wonders what if we could hear the sounds of eighteenth-century London? Indeed, what then? Do we really need more documentation of ourselves? And who would ever listen to those documents besides supernerds and PhD candidates? If many more cities and towns across the world were to compile their own sound surveys, preferably financed by the state budget, how wondrous that would be. Like preserving a natural resource, and then handing it over to the tourist bureau. That could even be part of the package tour: borrow a microphone, contribute to the sound survey. No one else has to listen.

Inner Listening

When we hear a stock phrase like Listen to your heart, what does that mean? Or, She listens to an inner voice. Can we hear it too? Or, Listen to your body. Indigestion aside, there's not much sound involved. The sound universe isn't the only sphere of listening, apparently. Is listening a metaphor, then, in such locutions? Not exactly. A question of focus, attention, tuning in; and also memory, listening to what we know, from experience, for clues about what we don't know. That suggests listening fits into a process of understanding: a listening that is both open and engaged. But are the ears not implicated in this listening? The ears may be a kind of mind, always sounding the world, for beauty and for danger and for where to go. This inner listening is looking for an inner lake where reflections set the surface world back into working order.

CONCERTGOING 7:
PARIS

To think of concerts seen, attended, heard; and if not of the music that we seldom can recollect, then of its circumstances as well as our own. We remember that we went, though memory makes sure to insert its errors. With some exceptions, the singularity of the event escapes us in the long run. The mind returns, as the body had done, to the venues or halls or intimate spaces that we frequented to hear such sounds. The atmosphere, the tone of those places remains with us, more than the musical organism that came into existence for a while that night or day.

After I moved to Paris, I went as often as I could to hear music, if it was free or affordable, and the more I looked the more I found. In my first months there, spring 1980, I saw the double bass player Maarten Altena do a solo concert at the Dutch Cultural Institute; the trumpeter and composer Bill Dixon, jazz pioneer from the 1960s, playing in a famous old *cave* on the Rue des Lombards; and Mike Zwerin's group at the American Center. I wrote about all those performances, among my first writings on music. So, see, listen, hear—for me—became see, listen, hear, write. Sometimes, at least. Enough to earn me a press card from *Jazz Forum*, the English-language journal of the International Jazz Federation, edited in Warsaw, and also from *Coda*, the jazz journal in Toronto. These cards got me into a certain number of concerts over the years, even if they did look a little homemade. But I continued to write about music all through the decade I lived in Paris. There was so much to listen to in that city, for me at that time, and it was the first place I'd lived where you could get everywhere by public transport.

That grand old three-story edifice with its garden on the Boulevard Raspail, long the residence of the American Center, was one of the places I frequented in those years. By summer, I was also going to the Dreher, a jazz club off the Place du Châtelet, which closed a year or so later. The club was in the basement, beneath the brasserie-café. I heard Steve Lacy's quintet there for the first time, and members of his group in another formation, and I think later still Lacy in duo with Mal Waldron. The World Saxophone Quartet played there too. I went to see them twice that week, but one time we got in with the band, Ali and me, since we were helping carry instruments downstairs to the club. Somehow he had engineered for him and me to take Julius Hemphill to a couscous restaurant, Le Casbah, in the crumbly neighborhood where I was living near the métro Pernety and from the same establishment to score some smoke for the distinguished saxophonist. From there, we took a taxi to the club.

But, I have to amend what I said before: we also, in a number of instances, don't remember that we went. I am certain there are many, many concerts we, I, don't recall having ever attended.

The next year, after I moved to the Rue Monge in the fall of 1981, I discovered the Dunois, a ground-level loft type of space down in the thirteenth arrondissement. In the years I went there, I saw many free improvisers from Europe and the US, always a challenge for listener and musician alike. I don't really remember most of it, but the list of people I saw would include Derek Bailey, Lacy, the Workshop de Lyon, Evan Parker, Joëlle Léandre, George Lewis, Lol Coxhill, the Rova Sax Quartet, Conny Bauer, Peter Brotzmann, and on. From my six-floor walkup near the Place Monge, I figured out a route strolling down through the fifth and into the thirteenth, following how the streets fed into each other all the way to the Rue Dunois. Most of the time I went alone, and inevitably there was a sense of excitement about the music we were all about to hear.

The club I frequented longest in those years was the New Morning, which opened in '81 and is still going strong. Up in the tenth arrondissement, on the Rue des Petites Ecuries (Street of Little Stables), it was a cavernous space once you got all the way inside, warmed up a bit by the poster-size blowups across the walls of African postage stamps honoring American jazz musicians. The New Morning featured some of the bigger acts. So, usually in the company of Ali, I got to hear a long fantastic roster of artists: Archie Shepp, Sam Rivers, Max Roach, Lacy's group, the Vienna Art Orchestra, Art Blakey, Mike Westbrook, Chris McGregor's Brotherhood of Breath, Charlie Haden's Liberation Music Orchestra, Cecil Taylor, Dizzy Gillespie, Toto Bissainthe, Mahlathini and the Mahotella Queens, not to mention Ali's own band, Sir Ali's Girls. And in about '86, Ali and I hung out with the legendary Prince Lasha between sets, sharing a joint with him as we walked up and down the street. Such lucky encounters—this was Paris! Nor did it escape my mind that we were just around the corner from Cortázar's last home (where I had interviewed him a few years earlier): I never saw him at the New Morning, but he might well have been there in spirit.

BOTHER

Noise annoyances. Can't you just *not* listen for once? How much longer are they going to be ripping boards at that house across the way? The food delivery truck out front idling with its giant refrigerator. Helicopter buzzing around overhead—want to swat it. Grating of the wooden footstool against the bathroom floor tiles, which only means her husband is reading on the toilet. Better to ignore it all. Uncle Howard's gas issues, especially when he's making tea. The girl who keeps catching the hiccups, it isn't funny, though it might start or end with laughter. Most irritating is that slight irregularity in the usual noise which surely is growing if you listen carefully—a wheel is falling off, the body breaking down, a collective madness catching fire, although it may also be nothing. Stop listening so hard. Always the same moaning through the wall next door. You didn't hear it. Or the inane voices from the TV, in another room somewhere, like a natural element, the persistence of insects. Cicadas lately, endless as a snow shower.

AUDIENCE

When some august personage ensconced on their throne grants an audience to a humble petitioner, we might call that an act of mercy or justice, or even self-preservation (the most reclusive despot must still *appear* to listen occasionally). To give a hearing, and presumably listen, to questions or complaints is to submit, if not to the start of a dialogue, then at least to the assumption of a response. That kind of audience, as a hearing, becomes transmuted only a little when we the public embody the hearing as an audience assembled for a particular moment's performance. An event—we watch and listen and attend. We the audience are the humble ones while the petitioner has been raised up onto a stage.

Yet the performer famously needs the audience more than the other way around. Perhaps musicians are the exception? Too often have I sat among an audience smaller than the group of musicians onstage, and I wonder for them how much does it matter? Sure, everyone prefers a full house, and it pays better, but the musicians are going to play regardless, given the opportunity—someone will be listening. Especially in a space like Roulette that can seat a couple hundred, when I myself have made up a substantial portion of the audience I feel almost as if we haven't done our part by being so few, while aware at the same time of our luck, having had the good sense to be there at a performance of such caliber. In New York—in Brooklyn!—we are very spoiled, big surprise. I wonder, in an audience of five or ten amid the many empty seats, if I listen differently to the music. Do I compensate for all the absences around me, listen to more of or in a bigger way? Something's affected, not sure what. But it is a luxury to enjoy that space on all sides of me when I go to a concert, to take it in grandly.

Of course, there is more intimacy when the numbers are small, and with the density of activity hereabouts that scale is becoming almost the norm. The last few years, within blocks of my house there have arisen three venues for mostly improvised music where twenty people make a full crowd. I lost the taste early for massive audiences; too intense, too noisy and distracting and distant. So, for me as a listener with a certain experience, this return to music in a room has been most welcome.

PRESENCE

Between listening, and hearing, and retention, and memory, all that in a constant and simultaneous loop, it's a wonder our bodies aren't fatigued just from the work our brains are doing every minute.

But is there a reflex for listening, before even the brain is engaged? Does the body know, in its own way, to listen?

A sense of the space around us, unencumbered by the fixative of words. We can intuit, hear, listen to our surroundings—where we happen to be—without reaching for the words to define it. Or so we do in working toward the words. And yet, if we bother to articulate the space through language, we are quickly reminded that doesn't nearly contain what we know.

What I am getting at, I suppose, is a feeling of presence. A sort of awareness, or listening, in the body. A physical reading of elusive facts. Inhabiting a space for however briefly, moving through that space. The brain can do all its fancy turns, so busy, but here you are anyway a while.

The Single Note

From the one, the many. That's really the oldest story. Science, religion, music: all arise from that basic principle. Paul McCartney once said how he could hear a whole song in one chord, and speculated that it might be possible to hear a whole song in one note if you were listening hard enough. Steve Lacy talked about a similar idea, but rather the importance for a musician sometimes to dwell on that one note and really go into it, exploring that note for all it's worth.

To seek the intimations of such a flowering from a single note, what powers of hearing or delirium does that require? Surely it would depend on what instrument produced the note and the character of the sound as it decays. Overtones, the possible clash of harmonics, the pulse and wavering within that solid note materialized out of thin air—these shape the sense of direction divined from that sound, the likely avenues of development and convergence. And yet it is still just one note: an egg, a rock, a prayer. A mystery to be settled either by its natural disintegration or the distinct personality of a dogged listener, gnawing at the bone of that sovereign note until it yields some clues.

Before the singularity, then, stands a savvy or deranged or inspired listener. Said listener is likely to be a musician, but it could be a *mélomane* like me stumbling upon that well of the note; long as they don't fall in, a tune might arise out of them too. As with a drone, a tonic, a modal anchor, we cannot take flight if we do not start from the ground. Clearly, all such flights carry a subjective impulse. The one note, absolute in itself, resonates a little differently in every listener. As we step inside the rim, we may project multiple branchings from that note, and hear them spin about in a kind of *folie*. If a form emerges, if our brief bout of madness proves resilient, takes a life of its own, we may even slap a name on it to find our way back there. Or, that single and sovereign note might simply fade before us, awash in its memory of the sounding.

To Others

Do you hear me? Are you listening at all?

Cart before the horse.

Do you hear yourself? Were you listening to what you've been telling us for the past couple hours?

That first question—"Do you hear me?"—carries a long, long history fraught with the most basic issues regarding human exchange. Issues so elemental they may determine the survival of humankind: respect, recognition, fairness.

But, in the current moment, at least where commerce and technology reign supreme in the US, that question has become so hollowed out as to effectively lose its meaning; or worse, converted into a pretext for bad behavior. In a common robocall tactic, the caller wields a seemingly innocuous variation: Hello? Can you hear me? Followed by a pause where the respondent can say anything at all, doesn't matter, for the recorded voice is set up to simulate an initial conversation that will soon lead to a sales pitch. In other words, who the hell cares, just stay on the line so we can sink our claws into your wallet. Exploiting the desire to make contact by this intrusion, the perpetrators seek only to catch us off guard.

The initial questions, though, are most relevant on an interpersonal level. A friend you don't see often invites you over for lunch. Not one of your closest friends who really needs to talk because a lot is going on with them, but simply to get together because it's been a while. So, you eat and drink and talk. Later, you realize—if you hadn't already—that this friend, whom you do like, and with whom you share a bit of history, hardly asked a single question about you and yours. When you volunteered some curious fact about your past, or a recent small accomplishment, or an upcoming voyage, it all vanished in the heap of unexamined paths. Instead, at every turn the conversation kept coming back to the friend, their achievements, their friends (some of whom you may know), their relationships, all the better if there is some second-hand prestige or celebrity dust to show off. I have known a few people like that—as if they showed up with their public face, ready for their close-up, rather than the private one that we fear might not exist at all.

That inability to listen, whether a temporary indisposition or a serious character flaw, poses an obstacle to the fundamental ecology of human growth. We assure ourselves that such friends are not always like that; maybe it's their reaction to us, for some reason, or their insecurities get the better of them occasionally. The resistance to listening, a sort of psychic blockage, may not be life threatening but it does hamper a healthy sense of being in the world. Listening keeps us upright, orients the lumbering creatures that we are so that we don't crash into others. I do not mean to privilege the obvious sonic aspects of listening exclusively, for the deaf can listen too, in their way, through sight and the other senses, since it is a matter of mind, of attention and awareness, as much as anything. We are not alone when we listen, and if we happen to become sufficiently absorbed in what (or whom) we are listening to, for that brief interval we may practically be liberated of our selves.

Getting back to those elemental issues, if I may be so bold as to generalize about the past half-millennium-plus, since the Christian West's voyages of discovery and conquest, the white man's burden turns out to be himself. If he had been able to listen to himself from outside his bloody certainties, he might not be in the mess he's in today. Or never mind that: if he had been able to listen to anyone else, he might have discovered something far more important, his humanity. By listening to an/other you become an/other for them; and so, together, you may understand you are the same.

Skin Listens

Poetic fragment found in an old notebook from over twenty years ago. Just the one page filled; the rest unused, waiting. Must have known, somehow, that I'd be writing this book one day.

> forms of listening.
> my daughter's arm over the edge
> of the bed at night
> arm knowing where the bed
> ends, skin against
> the surfaces adrum

But it's true that the skin listens. Consider the lovers whose bodies move as if in dialogue. We are each a walking, talking drum sounded by wind, sun, air, others' gazes, sounding in turn through the jungle of this world.

COMING BACK

As we awaken in the morning, and our body awakens—breathing, kidneys, bowels—how does our listening also awaken? Our bodily systems do not shut down exactly, nor really hibernate (one night is not an entire winter), so where does the listening go while we rest or wander in the submerged realm of sleep, where is it coming back from? Clearly we are permeable while lying there, sounds and voices do reach us sometimes; but our internal translator answers to no one in appropriating those chance discoveries, even if its purposes are determined on the fly. The sounds and voices that gain entry become incorporated into a new or altered context, and we are helpless, it seems, to impede their concatenations. The unconscious listens by its own lights, and always profits from its finds.

The small, quick increments of waking from sleep are often led, I think, by listening. All is distance outside ourselves, impenetrable distance, until that sentinel on the promontory of the ear catches wind of a signal that begins to gain clarity: the call of a bird or the bark of a dog, stirring of leaves, or the rude honk of a horn. We are here, it is day, we may not know which day yet or where here is, but we are in our bed, in our body, the long interval of flight or inexplicable absence is over, anchored once more by our listening that gathers up and reassembles the unassuming details of our life in the only world that we presume to know.

Familiar Voices

Roar of the crowd; we strain to listen to the person sitting next to us. Across the noisy street, no use trying: we cannot hear our friend who shouts and gesticulates in a pantomime of communication. The crackling phone line when we pick up—in the sonic hailstorm a familiar voice emerges just enough that we persist in a confounding effort at recovery. Such obstacles quicken our determination to listen through them, and still we may end up lost, grasping at the tatters of a connection. We don't need much to draw us on, no pied piper, just the glimmer of a voice we know, that knows us. We will plunge through darkness, through bewildering wreckage, for the sake of a voice.

The voices of those who have been close in our lives—parents, siblings, children, friends, teachers—stay with us. Even after a long absence, we would recognize them. Though the voices may change with time, as a face changes, and as our memories also may shift a little in our perpetual realignment with the present, nonetheless we would likely find our way back again. Those voices are like keys in the lifelong elaboration of our own music. A distinct and mysterious chemistry informs each of them.

The individuality we recognize, however, is predominantly language-bound. If someone we know or knew so well were to speak to us, unseen, in another language, one we understood but had never heard them speak, would we still be certain who they were? That is none too sure; it would be strange. And if in a language whose sounds were completely foreign? Probably not. Or, at any rate, that person long familiar will suddenly seem foreign too, as in a troubling dream. We want to be guided by our voices, comforted by them, tuned as we are to their pitches and cadences.

MUSIC AND TRAVEL

Well do we know that listening is a form of travel. But the experience of certain music, its imaginative pull, may animate the desire to go immerse oneself in the landscape, in the cultural terrain which gave rise to that music. We cannot help it, once engaged; we must do what we can to follow the scent, or forever feel that special longing.

For me, such enchantment has struck several times. In the last few years, Ethiopia was the goal, and I almost went but had to cancel at the last minute. The fever has subsided since then, though the wish remains and is easily stoked sometimes. For decades, I had had a sense of the uniquely fascinating history of the country, and even heard a bit of the music, enough to be intrigued. I have also enjoyed Ethiopian cuisine in a number of cities along the way. But about five years ago, friends in different places happened to give me copies of recordings by popular Ethiopian musicians from the 1960s, and I began to be hooked. These were early entries in the magnificent Ethiopiques series of mostly reissues produced by the French label Buda Musique, and a year or two after, I did a small translation job for the label by way of Ali. In lieu of a check, I asked if I might be paid with the full series of nearly thirty titles. Gilles, the generous owner, agreed and soon I was in possession of that treasure trove. In really soaking up those sounds, I became all the more intoxicated by their sensibilities, and began to feel I could hear the ancient trade routes that made up their distinct blend. Soon I wanted to go there, to hear what I could of that music in the place where it came from, and I asked a friend if he would like to travel with me. For months and months leading up to our departure, my readings in Ethiopia's political history and music history and culture as well as its current moment became almost a full-time occupation, nearly an obsession, and any friend who asked (or didn't ask) would get more than an earful on all I'd discovered already. Until; until the whole enterprise had to be put on hold, to be resumed before too long, I hope. Perhaps it's just as well to take a step back for a while, as if I'd developed a schoolboy crush on the Queen of Sheba that was only going to embarrass me.

But I also realize this process was not exactly new for me. Way back in my mid-teens, what else sent me traveling across America if not my recent adoption of a folkie esthetic? The sounds of the banjo first caught my ear soon after I moved to Berkeley at fourteen, and as I learned to play the instrument, above all from listening to many records and seeing live performers, I gained entry to a world well beyond my schooling (even as adventurous a place as Berkeley High School was at the beginning of the '70s couldn't take me to such realms). Through the music and songs and the particular camaraderie—and the old-timey style of banjo playing I favored, closer to its African roots and older than the flash and dash of bluegrass—I was discovering an America that I hadn't known before, a land bursting at the seams with life and stories and daily struggles, just the other side of the suburban daze that was more familiar to me yet never seemed quite real. So, by the time I finished high school, it was that America which called me, not the cozy slumber of colleges and universities, the natural next step for someone of my background. I wasn't thinking too hard about the future, but I knew that road could last me a lifetime. Yet I understood I could never be a professional musician—too much traveling just to survive. Even so, in that time, music propelled me across the land.

If listening itself is travel, that is because first it sends us dreaming. Whether music or voices, we respond by lending them our attention, letting them take us a certain distance. But as the experience rattles through our head, our attention wanders, poking down byways, mixing mystery and memories, getting lost, only to be nudged back to the matters at hand. For listening is implicitly a dialogue, even when one end of it is usually silent; we are there, regardless of where else we are. Undivided attention: was it ever thus, even before our over-stimulated times? And would we want our attention so undivided? What would be gained by that? In listening we yield to the impulse for departure, away from ourselves. We cannot help it if we wander past the object of our listening.

Regarding my initial point: a passion for the music of a place and time need not be the primary spark to animate our dream of travel. The other senses want to get in on the act too (amusing to imagine scenarios where touch is the impetus for a voyage). Argentina, where I will be visiting soon for the first time, did indeed drop into my radar by way of music some 45 years ago, after hearing Atahualpa Yupanqui (via recordings by Gordon Bok of Maine, originally), and Mercedes Sosa, and Gato Barbieri. Later, Piazzolla and other masters of the bandoneón like Juan José Mosalini and Dino Saluzzi captivated me with the special sonorities of that instrument, like a magic box of nostalgias that could not possibly be my own, although they felt like mine. But all that was fed and amplified by so many of the writers, along with friendships and long conversations, not to mention the indulgent delights of dulce de leche and the bountiful feast of grilled meat in a good *parrillada*.

On the other hand, that dream plucked from the branch and slowly converted into a plan, where once was a land I hardly knew existed—what I hope will be a trip to Iran next year or the year after, in time for Nowruz, Persian New Year, spring equinox—was first set into motion long ago by friendship. In my early twenties I was aware of the overthrow of the Shah and the Islamic revolution, and of the Americans' history of ruinous meddling around the world, but I had no personal perspective on its effects until I arrived in Paris at the same time as Ali, who was stuck there unable to return to art school in the States and who quickly became one of my closest friends. How was it, I wondered as I got to know him, that he came to many of the same musical tastes and watched some of the same TV shows, growing up in Tehran, as I did in Deal, NJ, and Berkeley? And if all those shared affinities gave some measure of the many Western imports to his land, what then of the far more vast and ancient native culture from which he came? Over the years, I read many books of literature and history and reportage, as well as books on Islam (he is no more religious than I am, which is to say not at all—we both eat plenty of pork). I also eagerly partook in the marvels of Persian cuisine, especially when his parents were visiting. And, inevitably my first line of research, I began to borrow every record I could find, in the Paris libraries, of classical Persian music, and often taped copies on cassette. Mysterious as those distinctive instruments have remained to my ears, their sounds have nonetheless grown a little bit familiar. Tar, setar, kamancheh, zarb, all still transport me decades later, but it was always the santur that charmed me the most, like a call to deep and drifting meditations. Perhaps that is also owing to its similarities with the larger hammered dulcimer, a fond discovery in my folkie days (I built one as a teenager, and three-quarters of another). Lately, Ali has met a number of Iranian musicians in Paris variously touching on jazz, and has just produced a record by one group. Persian elements remain front and center, but with many other influences filtered through them. So, we will have plenty of musicians to go visit whenever we do manage to get to Tehran.

EXPECTATION

If we go to a concert, usually we have at least some idea of what we will hear and who will be playing. Will it measure up to what we imagined? Naturally, our expectations vary according to the kind of music. If it's basically a live version of a record, then faithfulness to the product is paramount. But if the music is substantially improvised, the experience is bound to be more open, less defined; we are looking to chance upon something new, never quite heard before.

While the quiet drama of expectations unfolds along certain patterns in listening to live music, the subtleties of anticipation play out over a more complicated range before a first encounter with recorded music. Leaving aside the current commerce—or pirating, or generally free acquisition—of digital downloads, in the not so distant past when record stores still ruled the landscape, one entered such a shop with mixed emotions, as though in thrall to a vice that might prove beneficial if it doesn't lead to ruination. Those who went in for a specific item hardly knew the joys of doubt, fulfillment, disappointment; they sought the mere possession of a known quantity. The rest of us, though, tossing about in our distraction, laid ourselves open to inspiration or folly, anxious that our potential investment might turn out to be just more waste. In earlier decades, many record stores were set up to enable customers to listen to their stock, thus muting the perils and pleasures of anticipation. Still, there was often a winding path of curiosities and associations that led to the music chosen. Hearing the music or not before purchase, the prospect for gratification was not easy to gauge. Would you really care to listen to that record more than once or twice? In those days, each disc in a person's collection had to count for more, since most of us had fewer recordings then.

In the world of today, just about all recorded music is available anytime—an exaggeration only for those who still retain some memory or a capacity for research. Record stores (what few remain), especially used record stores, resemble the calling of a priest (or an elder in a cult), but without the perversion and cruelty. Still, the demands of the so-called marketplace persist in imposing an ever more precarious system of classification on music, abetted by a host of cultural prejudices that prefer to keep high and low in their places so that we may have some idea of what is worthy. Such ordering shapes our expectations, and some musicians do what they can to circumvent the boxes, at least until a certain resignation sets in. Thirty years ago, I engaged in a dialogue by correspondence for a season with Larry Ochs of the Rova Saxophone Quartet, who was seeking a new term for their music. I appreciated his concern and the avenues of his thinking—rather than a genre or style, he wanted to emphasize its nature as horn music—but I ended up assuming the unlikely role of Mr. Practicality and asked, Where would a person find Rova's records in a store? Because of the central role of improvisation in their music, the obvious answer was to file it under Jazz. But neither of us found that very helpful in describing the music. Perhaps the apparent need to de-scribe music is part of the problem, when it doesn't fit comfortably into well-worn styles, where the result of such effort is rather to pro-scribe what it is supposed to be in assuming a given label. Regardless of what readers of reviews might think they want, writers are probably more useful when they seek to convey what is active in a particular music rather than how a sense of its lineage places it in a certain taxonomy.

Label turns out to be the operative word here. Most small and mid-size record labels articulate a particular identity, reflecting their owners' tastes, whims, obsessions, if not a determined mission. Even where the music slips past easy casting, familiarity with a label may frame expectations, so that we as listeners know what sensibilities have a home there. But it's not always so simple. For almost a year, I have been on the list of a Norwegian label that has sent me some twenty CDs. Ali encouraged me to make contact, after playing for me a record by a woman trumpeter that was really quite special, above all her tracks on goat horn. However, while I will keep a few discs, with each new shipment of CDs my vague expectations were stymied, scrambled, readjusted. Most releases were just not that unique to my ears (no doubt this can be said of many record labels). The musicianship, I recognize, was of a consistently high standard, yet it did not linger in my mind. Just a few had something as singular as the woman on goat horn—not as novelty, but as sound and expression—and these I was not likely to find anywhere else. One might be tempted to ask: What is Norwegian jazz-related music "supposed" to sound like? Are there inherent northern qualities, whatever that means? Unhelpful questions. Moreover, many of the label's releases included musicians from elsewhere—South Africa, Mozambique, Brazil, Italy, France, the US, Japan—and some were recorded at its other studio, in Valencia, Spain. If these too scrambled expectations, a laudable impulse overall, and if the label clearly intended to not be easily regionalized, it all left me sonically a bit lost. Surely this was due in part to my own complex expectations: place does not necessarily determine style; and, when you've got as many CDs as I do, you need a good reason to keep anything new. Finally, I wrote to the label's kind owner, thanking him, and suggested he spare himself further expense and take me off his list, or at most send me only his oddest releases.

Beyond Identity Markers

The question remains elusive, and perhaps it's irrelevant, but it has to be asked: Is listening conditioned by racial, ethnic, gender, sexual, even class factors? How would that work? How could the reductionist constructs of race possibly illuminate or determine the process of listening, which is inherently a human faculty? *What* we choose to seek out and focus on is another matter, affected by any and all such factors, as they affected the cultures that nourished us as we grew. But do a Mongolian, a Maori, a Bushman, an Azeri, a Roma, a Sami, a Lakota Sioux really listen differently from each other? And as to the *what*, it really comes down to the individual in the end, that distinct set of ears and mind, of antennae, who will always reach past what the culture provided, at least a little, thus enabling their culture to continue to grow. So, the *what* can be anything. The conditions that formed us do not tell us *how* to listen; we learn to figure out that part for ourselves, a learning without end even for the least curious among us. Where others have told us we must listen, or must not, that sooner provides fodder for our resistance, occasions to question. Regardless, there are no doubt essentialists who would argue that women do indeed listen differently than men, that a very rich person and a very poor person are not equipped to listen in the same way, even that a black person and a white person somehow differ in that respect. Such superficial distinctions leave me unconvinced, for these are all ultimately beside the point in anyone's apprenticeship of listening. Our ears lead us where they may, we cannot help but wander off the beaten track sometimes. Anything at all might catch our attention given the right circumstances, and no statistical or genetic classification will define how we open ourselves to the world nor who we are that does the listening.

Concertgoing 8:
New York

How to account for twenty-eight years of listening to music in New York, almost a blur. So many, many performances; in clubs, spaces, theaters, museums, bars, homes, parks, churches—and I can hardly recall the concerts from last month. I will have to consult my agendas for those early years, to see what I forgot. But I do notice a progression of sorts in the places where I have lived. From the Jersey shore to Berkeley to LA to Paris and then to New York, the opportunities for listening expanded for me exponentially. And in the past decade now, Brooklyn itself has provided most of my musical sustenance.

What is it about the lure of live music, live performance, being in the moment, with its risk of collapse and its promises, that we always have to have more? Why do we need this thing, this almost nothing, such that we go again and again in search of it? And take nothing away but the experience. Where music is offered, we go there to listen, that's all, not to read the paper or climb on a ladder, and to watch the people making that music. Whatever the space, and with the singularity of each particular space, the experience is different than listening to a recording. It's a way of adding to what we've heard, even surprising us; we want to be surprised somehow, that is also why we attend. Because we don't know how that specific group will sound that night.

So, it should not seem unexpected that a kind of amnesia settles over us soon after we leave the hall where the music took place, after it has rinsed loose from the stones and the trees and the air. Nothing more to listen to. Just a memory full of holes, and the vague certainty of where we were but a moment ago. Yet somewhere the embers remain of that music, still dimly aglow, added to all the others. There may be some residue that persists, likely beneficial, because after all it was music that passed through us, human spirit, and something beyond the human.

Some of what I recall, glimpses, is because I had to work a little more for the experience, in that I was writing about it. Two pieces for the *Village Voice*, my first year in New York, 1989, were instances of writing I had never done before and so my listening, how I took it all in, was like an experiment as well. I can't even say if my listening was different except that I had an immediate purpose which demanded some form of increased attention. I had to write my article right after the concert—which I had done in the past, but in a more casual way. I was never a full-time journalist, the pieces I wrote didn't require an immediate turnaround between the experience and the published text. But if I wanted to consider pursuing such a line of work, I better get used to it. My first piece for the *Voice*, I went over to the Knitting Factory on East Houston to catch Khan Jamal, the vibes player from Philadelphia. I really liked what I'd heard of his Steeplechase records. Ali and I both started listening to him after his first record with Johnny Dyani in the mid-1980s. And I was sitting at a table right in front of the stage with my not yet wife, jotting notes as I was listening. I enjoyed it plenty, but what did I hear? I'll have to go back and read my own article.

A month or two later, first day of summer, I had to get down to the tip of Battery Park before dawn. There, with a keyboard slung around his neck, was Sun Ra, plus Don Cherry with his pocket trumpet, and five members of the Arkestra, all about to lead a procession in celebration of the solstice. Produced by sound artist Charlie Morrow, with his bowler hat and blowing on a conch shell, the procession followed a short ways along the park overlooking the harbor until we settled into seats for the rest of the concert. I had gotten up around four in the morning, so I was wide awake by then, and I recognized this was really quite a special event, with such important figures in music. But how, I surely wondered even at the time, did Sun Ra, in his mid-70s, agree to perform at that hour? Did Charlie Morrow have a large grant to finance the event? As usual, Sun Ra had us going with his catchy space ditties and all the rest. It was remarkable that two hundred people could show up like that at the break of day, and I was always delighted to hear Don Cherry in any group, he enhanced whatever was going on, gave it extra spirit.

Which is why I recall the last time I went to a Don Cherry concert, in the mid-1990s up at Symphony Space, less than a year before he died. Because he didn't play much at all, and as a result the band, disciples mostly, wasn't up to a whole lot. Whether he was drugged out or what, he tended to float on the music more than engage with it. Something was not right, that much seemed clear.

EAR TO PAGE

I listen to the words on the page. That is how the writing advances, like a fresh spring running where the terrain yields, where inflections of resistance in earth and rock push it forward, away, turning, and turning again headlong. Except: writing is not as easy as water, and not half so mindless, even when lost in the flow. For me, the articulation of language into a sequence of phrases and thoughts, however continuous or disrupted, is engineered by a process of listening, as if the inner ear with its weights and measures for the subtlest values, its instincts for balance and the limits of movement, were the true master of the dance. The subjects of that writing, its themes and intentions and intellectual bluster, or simply its merest ambitions as a beauty contestant, will show little grace if the ear is not tuned in.

There are, of course, dangers in falling for lines that "sound good." We can be charmed by our own sweet talk, lulled by pleasant sensations into relaxing our critical faculties. So, the ear that sounds out the words and phrases as they unfold bears a kind of responsibility—a duty to listen twice, as it were—lest the enticements of the language encourage deception. But then, as we already know, such purposes are all around us. What that responsibility implies, therefore, is a moral question: are we, with our pretty talk, trying to deceive (others or ourselves)? Never mind whether people prefer the illusion. Were we not supposed to dazzle our audience into surrender?

It is a mysterious process, that listening, not quite religious or prophetic, but deeply human. We can't be sure we get it right. Language as a form of music—or the other way around—dwells like a subterranean force within us, and our listening slowly draws it out. In divining that spirit, impelled by whatever spark has befallen us at the right moment, we are driven less by the aim of a determined message than the need to discover how it sings to us and perhaps to others as well.

In-between Sounds

Taking a breath. Like when I'm swimming, every third stroke: a breath. Audible only to me as I move, head turned, until my face meets the water again. Or the horn player, blowing a stream of notes, who for the briefest moment lets go the mouthpiece enough to pull in a mountain of air, making barely a rasp, a clasp flying open and shut, the quick interval for breath soon forgotten. Those quiet interstitial sounds, when noticed, skate the edge of necessary information; we let them float away without a thought. There must be fields upon fields of such sounds, swept aside by the weight of circumstance, habit, focus.

If some in-between sounds we scarcely register, others simply shouldn't be there. That much is clear as soon as we hear them. The person who reads—or worse, prays—out loud. Don't they get it? Did they not learn properly? And then this, an occupational hazard or a bad habit that some teacher neglected to purge: the instrumentalist, often a pianist, who hums along or sort of sings as they play. Some audiences love it, impressed or charmed by so much immersion in the act of making music. But many of us would sooner listen past the vocalizing, if we like the musician otherwise, straining it out like an unavoidable flaw. And still it goes on, the humming-singing, even straying from the lines, an unruly lock of hair. I become conscious of the effort to ignore it, while reminding myself this is the price sometimes of beautiful things. But I would prefer not to hear it.

ROULETTE RIVER

Like a local watering hole for a seasoned drinker, the new music and experimental media venue Roulette has been my go-to place for the past four or five years. Should I have called it my listening hole, to further the analogy? Sounds weird, even perverse. Co-founded by trombonist Jim Staley and others almost forty years ago, located mostly in one and then another Soho loft (the later spot, on Greene Street above Canal, I visited on various occasions: I caught Larry Ochs and Donald Robinson's duo, Steve Swell's avant big band, and the final event there, a take on Mauricio Kagel's exuberant and Dadaistic music-theater works), Roulette moved to Brooklyn in 2012; they raised a lot of money and city support and also much debt, to renovate the old ground-floor theater and mezzanine in a YWCA building on Third Avenue at the corner of Atlantic, where the rest of the twelve floors are still a women's residence building. From their first season in the new home, I saw not just that I should support them but that their schedule was sufficiently packed with concerts I would attend, so that I should join at the full all-access level, $250 a year, which granted entry to all their productions. Even from a purely economic point of view, it was no contest. Each year I've gone to some thirty concerts there.

I had passed the building for years, when driving my kids to school. I have always found parking on Atlantic within a block or two of Roulette, and that's about the same distance from the closest subway station, just two stops from my home. I had never before been a member of a concert-presenting organization, or not on that level. What did it mean to be able to go to any event? For one thing, I went to a lot more, didn't hesitate, except for my usual reluctance to leave the house. But it also encouraged what might count as a bad habit: nearly half the time I arrive there late, five or ten minutes after the music has started, even half an hour. Once in a while, I also leave before the end. Circumstances, sure, finishing dinner or washing dishes before heading out, but that access—and the fact of not buying a ticket to an individual event, with its attendant responsibility to use it—meant an open door, I could come and go as I liked. It might well be argued that such freedom and availability has the potential for a detrimental effect, in the way that we can be too casual about our blessings. Possession can make us lazy; we may fail to appreciate what seems to always be on offer, like a book that remains unread on our shelf for years. From that perspective, perhaps we forget the singularity of the event, imperfections and all.

But no sense being an alarmist either. The privilege bestowed on me as a member and supporter of Roulette also holds a more miraculous aspect. If, not infrequently, I arrive there late, it is through no intention of disrespect, nor any lack of recognition as to the unique character of an evening. Rather, my privilege grants access to a sort of lovely illusion as well. It is as if all the music performed there, year in and year out, comprises one large river, the Roulette river, and we may come to dip in its waters or sit on its banks almost anytime. And as long as we remember to treat it right, that river will continue to flow on and on.

Incomprehensible Understanding

Natural as it may be, listening takes some effort. Like walking or talking—except those can be done without paying attention. Listening, if in an active way, is paying attention and even venturing to engage. The effort is felt all the more when engaging in another language, one learned after childhood and thus always brandishing its obstacles. So, on our recent visit to Buenos Aires, I was listening up a storm, which didn't tire me out so much as keep my mind buzzing and busy.

Amid everything else, I gave three talks there, and that meant not just added listening but listening in public. Talking, after all, being impossible without listening. My Spanish was pretty good, but still one wonders. Two of the talks, in university settings, were almost dialogues: on both occasions, a *porteña* writer helped guide my talk with questions. Of course, none of this is unusual, except for me as an American raised (like most) in a single language—listening to other tongues was never a skill prized by my native culture.

In fact, that is how you get off your island, by listening. Whatever I had thought to say at the events in Buenos Aires, prior to sitting in that chair there in front of people, had to be reconfigured in the moment as a response to a question. So, the question was like a door being opened and listening carried me through that door. All around us the air, the land, the sea is teeming with questions, except we cannot hear them, fortunately, it would be too much. Listening draws them in one by one, or in clusters, sketching a path forward out of ourselves, out into the world. Somehow listening makes the questions audible, like a voice in a crowd, in that they take form in our consciousness as we become aware that the voice may well be speaking to us. For the questions to traverse another language in reaching us, or even not questions but the simple accompaniment of a voice, our listening forgets what we do not know, even that we came from another place. All communication is imperfect, it turns out, as those closest to us will continue to remind us. And sometimes we have to brave a great distance in order to understand what is being said.

HEALERS

A person employed in the care and maintenance of certain machines cannot hope to accomplish the task without a trained ear. How many times have we taken our car to a mechanic, they listen a few moments, and come up with a diagnosis? Presumably they hear the same sounds we do; but they know how to read them, while we can hardly advance beyond saying "that doesn't sound right." I came up with the same brilliant conclusion the other day when trying to get an external disc drive to work with my new laptop. Likely a problem of software, but I heard the stuttering mechanism as a failure to engage, to read the disc, because that much I thought I recognized from the fickle disc drives in other devices. "Doesn't sound right" may indeed be a long way from being able to divine the particulars. The smooth running of an engine or a motor or any mechanical contraption, that much we can hear. But to discern the pathologies that may develop, the alphabets of friction, from the processes of a specific kind of machine takes some education, and above all the familiarity of experience. That car mechanic has heard hundreds, thousands of such engines; he or she knows those sounds better than their own child's breathing. Doctors too, of course, with and without stethoscopes, must learn to listen, whether or not it suits their personality. But bodies as well as people also lie, and so the doctor has to hone a special instinct for listening past deceit, even if that takes them onto shaky ground. Through listening, if we are not too impatient, we are likely to know far more than we realize.

What a mechanic or a doctor tries to do by listening into the problem at hand is not much different from the so-called whisperers (dog, horse, dolphin). The implication for those apparent miracle workers is that they know how to talk to animals where the rest of us do not; or to especially troubled animals. But that means they appreciate both the general characteristics of the given species as well as the unique variations of the individual. Talking to animals, however, as to people, is not an isolated act. A richly developed capacity for listening, even beyond human terms, is paramount. How did they learn how to listen to such animals? Who knows, they had teachers (including the animals themselves) or they figured it out somehow, but as with any listening the learning is never finished. To whisper, in such circumstances, is a sign of humility, a suggestion rather than a decree, almost a form of listening in the very act of speaking. The intimacy of the whisper is like a confession: for your ears only, you and me, here in this moment. That the animal is also listening, we could nearly take for granted, but there is the real breakthrough. The creature, convinced by experience of the less than stellar nature of the human species, though probably unaware of the monstrous exaggerations of the self, nonetheless responds by listening to the individual's calming voice and proffered hand. We might even say the animal takes pity on the whisperer, confirming the efficacy of their listening and thus exalting their humanity.

Whence and Whose

Improvised music with its being-in-the-moment, its perpetual existence in the present, shows a curious relation to historical time. Even so, as saxophonist Luis Conde notes in a recent blog post, there is an abundant past to this music—its history of perpetual presents, a present that never repeats itself exactly but constantly multiplies with infinite variations. Taking his example of Peter Brotzmann, having discovered a video of Brotzmann playing in the late 1960s and wondering how Brotzmann of today would hear that, it is rather as if there were thousands of Brotzmanns, each one in his moment, his actuality. So, we might inquire about that long road of present moments, why do they not form a real past—a terrain of memories, a history—of improvised music? Of course, the essential experience for the listener is to be there in the moment in which the music is produced, yet what do so many documents and recordings of this music, in its multiple presents from the past, reveal to us? Does listening to a given record revive that particular present now in the past, lift the cloak of oblivion from that which happened already?

Since we do live in time (so it seems), I wonder if some

movement can be detected, some advance, in improvised music. Is there some intellectual or esthetic acquisition, some understanding, which determines that this music in the current day is clearly different? It seems to me, generally, the answer is no. Or if there is, it's to be found rather on the personal level. The Steve Lacy who came to Buenos Aires in 1966 and with his group recorded *The Forest and the Zoo*, on the 8th of October of that year, never again made music as free as that; it remains a period in the search for his own style where he could best provide a frame for the improvisation, to contain the maximum possibilities. Leaving aside his own trajectory, to my ears a music like that could be made today as well. There are new ways of thinking up a context for making improvised music, new structures and processes, but the idea of scientific progress does not translate easily to the arts. Improvised music is a practice, almost a rite (but without so much solemnity, as is fitting for a practice of spontaneity and which values humor), as much for musicians as for listeners. And it's not a matter of old folks; this practice continues to interest young musicians everywhere.

Whether or not it has a sense of the past, or memory, another angle from which improvised music can be examined comes down to this: Where is it located? Or, where do the musicians come from and can something of their origins be heard in their music? When Louis Moholo and Marilyn Crispell did a concert, was it obvious simply by hearing that one came from South Africa and the other from the United States? Not especially. Sure, sometimes we can guess where a certain way of playing arises from, but that soon ends up a rather dubious exercise. Luis observes that "current practices of improvisation derive from certain American or European experiences . . . from the sixties," all right, and there are clearly tendencies in the style of improvising, above all collectively, that differentiate the Germans from the Dutch and from the English; but, can we compare in the same way the Americans, the Argentines, the Italians, and the Swedish? Maybe in some cases, but each time it becomes more difficult, more complicated, and to what end? Geography and nationality, like religion and any other identity, say very little about the person inside just as they cannot say much about the improvised music that comes out of that person. And if this music is not really defined by a place (neither of its making nor in where its practitioners are from), does it therefore come out of a no-place and does that make it utopian?

Background Noise

A quiet place in the woods, so I imagined. Turns out to be a hundred yards from the highway. The steady wash of the cars (glimpsed discontinuously through the trees), a sort of liquid hum, can be abstracted into the distant roar of ocean waves, but only in the right measure of distraction. Mostly I don't pay attention, though it is always there in the air, even at night. Can we stop hearing a noise, once we are aware of its constant presence? It helps that the noise fluctuates a bit, and that the distance softens it. But even if we always hear it on some level, can we manage *not* to register its presence? City living is made up of many such compromises, subconscious negotiations with the teeming world around us; in the woods, our expectations are different.

This morning, I took a walk among the snowy roads of the property as far from the highway as they would take me. Wherever I went, the noise was still there faintly, like a sonic sky that could not be avoided. If forests are the lungs of the world, helping to clean the air left foul by bungling humans, what can neutralize the noise? Odd to think that technology would be the only solution to rid us of the waste products of technology. I've read occasionally about research into noise-canceling devices on a community-wide scale; the principle, as I recall, is computer-driven, taking a sort of imprint of any given noise and projecting in some way a reverse imprint that would indeed neutralize the sound, reduce it to—what? Dust? Silence? Can noise X plus anti-noise X possibly equal silence? Surely some residue would remain; the merest trace, a sound smudge.

Of course, we adapt, we live with the noises in our vicinity, render them undisturbing somehow. The wonders of our strange internal coping mechanisms, a mystery even to ourselves. But how do the many millions of people who live close to highways and airports and train tracks and industrial sites and ports and military bases and busy city streets manage to pretend the noise doesn't affect them? Would a researcher find their ears physically altered internally, with some kind of filter perhaps (imagine the evolutionary horrors that could lead to), or do their brains flip a switch that says it's just another wall out there but in that wall is a window and even a door? Sound penetrates, as we know, and studies have been made that map out the relation of noise, different kinds and intensities of noise, to stress and anxiety in the body. Granted, noise is often a subjective concept and hardly monolithic in its characteristics, but our reflex to domesticate it kicks in quickly. Usually, we mask one noise with another, friendlier sound—music, or radio—and when that's done, there it is again, same as ever. Those who suffer from the noise are merely collateral damage from the unstoppable momentum of civilization, or human restlessness. And yet, their adaptation is also our own, those of us who are more fortunate: if we actually listen to anything too constantly, even the most sublime music, we will likely go crazy all the same.

SOUNDS AUTHENTIC

Which are more easily deceived, the ears or the eyes? No doubt we are eager to be fooled sometimes: the trompe l'oeil painter and the sound effects artist find willing participants in the fun. But in music, listeners prove quite adept at letting their own illusions shape how they take in what they're hearing.

Questions of authenticity do have their place, however unstable; yet such questions may end up misleading in turn, posing traps of simplistic thinking. Can white people sing the blues? Do they have a right to? Don't be silly. But what about me, there I was at fifteen or sixteen up on stage singing that beautiful and haunting lament "Oh Death," after the great Appalachian banjo player Dock Boggs. I loved that song, yet what did I know about death? No one close to me had died, nor had hardly anyone I ever met. I performed the song in public several times back then, and nobody told me I shouldn't sing it. Still, the image of teenage me, an upper middle-class Berkeley lad, wailing away on that lament seems incongruous. I was not a morbid kid, nor remotely Appalachian; even so, I thought I felt that song in my bones.

Puzzling out what is or is not authentic in a performance,

and our assumptions about what that means, seems most salient an issue in the presence of vernacular styles, roots music, when we behold someone from outside that culture playing the music as if, with eyes closed, you wouldn't know. Though I never saw them play, many years ago I heard a tiny bit of a Japanese bluegrass band. How was it possible? Were they pure imitation? But they were kicking up the hay like the best of them. And never mind white blues musicians, how could a Frenchman, Bill Deraime, get away with playing the blues in French? Yet, why not? Maybe such phenomena are not so different from the folk revivalists of the '60s, many of whom had little or nothing of the musical culture they adopted in their own family backgrounds. Or the klezmer revival of the '70s and later, a good number of those musicians couldn't have been further from the original culture growing up in their American suburbs. Let alone to see clarinetist Don Byron playing that music in his early years, an African-American artist known later for his ambitious work in and out of the jazz tradition; or more recently, the klezmer players in Puebla, Mexico, none of whom are Jewish. Or what about the contemporary Argentine freak folk band Diente de Madera playing American traditional songs like "The Cuckoo"? Didn't any of these musicians get the memo? This was not their music! Shouldn't their listeners know?

TALKING TO OURSELVES

We all, let's face it, talk to ourselves sometimes—preferably when we're alone. So, if I were a sound artist, this is a piece I would like to make; better yet, I would like to listen to such a piece, let that hypothetical artist do the making. At a monastery, a convent, an artists' colony, or some retreat where guests have their own rooms, propose to all willing participants that you will place a voice-activated microphone in each person's quarters, assuring them somehow that their anonymity will be preserved; you yourself won't know who is who. It may be necessary to build in a placebo effect, or else a mechanism for activating different mikes at random, so that no one would know who is being recorded or when. That is, working with the assumption that everyone should be granted the opportunity for consent beforehand; the ideal would be for them not to know at all but that's not possible. If they think they are being recorded, that will encourage them either to put on a performance, to speak to the mike, or else to shut up completely. For them to make a game of it defeats the purpose; the object being to capture what they say to themselves in unguarded moments. If they can't be entirely unaware of the setup, then it should be arranged in whatever way best encourages them to forget about the hidden presence of the microphone. Maybe no recording should be made during the first days of their residency.

So much for engineering the situation. It's rather like trying to take photos or make recordings of wild animals while eliminating (removing, concealing) the human presence. As for the material produced, I think it is of no interest to retain, on the one hand, rote recitation of prayers to whatever god or, on the other hand, the sounds of unexpected sexual activity. What is singular about talking to oneself is that the voiced lines often surface before the speaker realizes, as if their subterranean dialogue or a train of runaway thought had suddenly become audible. The subject, the character, doesn't matter, and it may be just as surprising in its banality as in its cheekiness. We might almost liken it to hearing one side of a phone conversation, though with obvious differences. Now, what does our hypothetical sound artist do with all these solo voices, how might they be composed? That is where the artist is not just a technician, but I think the lines and voices harvested would naturally suggest their own possibilities of ordering. Sequences, juxtapositions, simultaneous groupings, repetitions, symmetries and asymmetries, beginnings and endings. It would take some playing around, there could be multiple versions as to demonstrate the fluidity of sense, a sort of rhyming or rhythmic principle might even be employed. And I, the listener, would enjoy them all.

My Name Is

What is your name? My name is. These are among the first phrases we learn in a new language. We want to know how to address people, and we want them to know who we are. To some extent, we are who our name is—even if we use several names or variants; even if some people know us by one version, and others by another; even if we use pseudonyms, as certain writers and criminals like to do. And every person has their own involuntary associations with our name, so that for one we trigger the briefest recall of an ex-lover, for another a mysterious cousin, and for another a boxer or a ballet dancer glimpsed on television as a child. In effect, the sound of our name, even the thought of the sound of our name, makes us slightly different people for each person who knows us or knows of us. And then some see fit to take liberties with our name, almost as if they can't help it, and will persist unless sternly discouraged. I have known Stevens and Jeffreys who are never Steve or Jeff. My father was Morris and hated the faux familiarity of Morrie, as if someone was looking to sell him something. Some friends occasionally call me Jas, though I have never encouraged it, but I don't bother to make an issue of the matter. (What is it about American culture that leads so many people to cut down names to one syllable when at all possible? The country is huge; isn't there room for two syllables, even six or eight? Or is it the endemic amnesia that our culture breeds, at least in native English speakers?)

Identity takes a further loop or several when placed in the context of other languages. My friend Luisa will hear her name more or less the same most anywhere she goes, though the people who pronounce it will have a somewhat different set of associations according to their culture. She once introduced me to a nephew or great-nephew of Buñuel, who is still the only person I ever heard of in Spanish with the same name as me. He pronounced it as one would in his language, where three of the five letters sound differently than in English and the accent falls on the second syllable instead. In French, where I have known of no one else with my name, the inclination would be to pronounce four of the five letters differently. Who am I, then, in those languages? The question gets all the more entangled: over the years, I couldn't decide how to pronounce my own name when introducing myself to people in French or Spanish. At first, I tended to follow their pronunciation rules, though as if with a question mark in my mind, until finally I resolved to just say it as I do in English. But that too sounded odd, when all the other words spoken followed different rules, thereby posing a double confirmation of my foreignness. That whiff of the foreign had been with me ever since childhood, in suburban New Jersey, since back then I knew of no one with my name except a man older than my parents. For a while, I wished I had a normal name like Bob. And often enough when someone first met me, even later occasionally in Paris, on hearing my name they apparently thought it quite clever to make reference to the Golden Fleece. As it happens, I have little memory of my exploits in those faraway lands—it was all so very long ago—but I know that in Greece, where I have actually never been, they pronounce my name differently yet again.

In the Air

In the air; in thin air. To vanish into thin air. What does that mean exactly? To vanish before one's eyes, all right, but why *thin* air? Is that like being at a high altitude where the air is thin due to less oxygen? And why would that affect visual phenomena? When it is said that an idea, a trend, a phrase is in the air, what is the nature of that conveyance? Aren't most ideas in the air, more or less in circulation, and if we all breathe the same air... or don't we? If sound requires oxygen to travel, does it fade away more quickly at high altitudes? Is there really no sound in space? What would an audio recording in space yield? Does humidity in the air alter sound? I haven't ever noticed that it does. Do fish hear in water? Water, after all, does have oxygen. We know that sea mammals hear in some way, or is it just that they *feel* sound waves down under? And what would be the difference? Or do they surface not just for air, but to have a chat sometimes? The air is mysterious enough. We cannot see it, cannot hear it, only its movement; and we cannot see or hear what makes it move. Sounds slip into the air (where were they before?), and are propelled through the air, but can they go home again? Or is home just a biological notion? Sounds have a physical existence, but no biology? Is sound not a form of life that also requires oxygen? Sound has a life of its own, in the air; and if not, then what are we listening to?

LESS PREPARED

I never would have thought it possible in earlier years. Or if doable, then ill-advised, presumptuous. How could I go interview a writer if I didn't know their work, at least in part? What would we talk about, what could I ask, and where follow? The fact is, I have always been able to find questions to ask people, anyone, if they let me, though discretion usually wins out. Even so, it's a good idea to do your homework to some extent—and yet I came to realize there can be value in not knowing too much, just enough to feed the desire to know more.

The circumstances of my experiment were a matter of limited time and maximum encounters. I was working on a book, under the guise of a doctorate, about Latin American writers in Paris. Contrary to academic trends, I was not placing their work, the written texts, at the indisputable center of my concerns; rather, I wanted to know as much as possible about the history of that relationship, the lives, the lore, and the varying dynamics of a foreigner's perspective, which in a few cases included changing languages. Since my interest was in what they experienced as much as what they produced, I knew my research had to include interviews with as many people as I could arrange to meet. With the contingencies of visiting Paris in summer and coordinating daily schedules with my wife and our two small kids (in 1997), not to mention remaining available for whenever one of a dozen or more writers might propose to meet, it required a lot of preliminary listening, as it were, just to set up each formal occasion for listening. There was not always time, consequently, to gather more than a few details in advance about the person; to locate their books, often published abroad, let alone carve out the hours to read them, was just not possible sometimes. Besides, I knew I was likely overreaching; I would hardly have room to fit them all in my book, given the quantity of past writers I wanted to discuss as well.

The extent of my not being prepared was relative, therefore; it did have an overall context. But my approach stood in contrast to the interviews I had done with writers ten or fifteen years earlier, when I read every book I could find by the writer and compiled copious pages of notes and questions, hoping not to sound too ignorant or naïve. I myself had more experience now, I was older; and my listening, in turn, was more seasoned. I don't know if that made any difference at all, though, for instance when I went to meet the Paraguayan ambassador to France in his office—a poet and short story writer and Guaraní scholar who had been imprisoned back in the 1960s and early '70s during his country's forty-year dictatorship. I knew scant details about him, his country's historic defeats, the centrality of its indigenous language, and I had only read a few passable translations of his poems in anthologies long before. But somehow that was enough as a point of departure to take matters further. He could see I wanted to know more: I had questions, and questions after that. I also understood that the willingness to listen, especially for an American to listen, goes a long way. The more we ask, it seems to me, the more we are humbled, as if there might be no end to the asking. I had worried, with that interview, that my lack of grounding in his intellectual labors might result in an encounter of little substance. But I think we did get at something resonant, precisely because I came from outside. I wonder further, since then, how that sort of qualified unknowing might carry us to other dialogues, toward new recognitions, new families.

CONCERTGOING 9:
BIG BANDS

The blast of the horns lifts me up every time, more than I might imagine. Even heard on record, a big band will have that effect on me; but to feel the full force of a live performance, the air thunderous with all that blowing, limbs and sinews, blood and breath stirred to attention, how can we not be changed by the experience? The exquisite machinery of a big band when it's blazing away, the players unafraid, each their part in the edifice of glory, transports me before I know it. We go marching forth in step, fortified by the joy in the music.

Is there such a thing as joy in music? For listeners like me, at least, and players too, what else to call it? That insubstantial something that seeps right to our core. And the music can be any size, any tone, when it seizes us. But a big band nearly overwhelms—there too is its power— so many Gabriels with their horns proclaiming fealty to a sound, a promise.

In the early 1980s, when I first saw Chris McGregor's Brotherhood of Breath in Paris, probably at the New Morning, only then did I really appreciate the special excitement of a big band. Amplified in his music were the lovely lilting South African melodies, the multileveled voicings. Eight or nine horns (brass and reeds), piano (McGregor), bass, and drums, the Brotherhood was a revelation to me. Rhythmically driven, very swinging, far reaching—and not American. After a dozen years, just a nucleus of the band was South African, but the music's origins were unmistakable, even with Europeans, and Caribbeans, and also Americans in the group; and even with echoes of Ellington and Basie, Mingus, Sun Ra, sounding through. The Brotherhood was always thrilling, and I played their records over and over, especially the more unbridled editions of the band from the '70s. Surely I saw them more than twice, with Ali, but I know the last time was outside at La Villette, on 3 July 1988, part of a festival there. In the open air that afternoon, their big band sound was like a great affirmation, a shout and dance for life, and that worked for me too since I had gone to hear them with my best friends. So, we were not disappointed: they delivered what we went there for.

It was in the '80s that I also got to see Sun Ra and his Arkestra, at least a couple times. Again, probably at the New Morning, but a more unusual venue was later at the Warsaw Jazz Jamboree in October 1987, at the spacious Sala Kongresowa behind the massive Palace of Culture and Science, a gift from Khrushchev. What a treat to behold the full complement of Sun Ra's crew in their glowing and colorful robes as they danced and chanted onto the wide stage—the rapt audience may not have known what to make of his Arkestra even at that late date. Someone I spoke with thought it was all an elaborate goof, that he was putting one over on the Polish public, but Sun Ra had been developing his sense of spectacle since the '40s. Far from a joke, his marvelous vision offered the audience a hopeful perspective on the future by using the popular language of the space age while also having fun. And when the Arkestra came together on one of their rousing themes steeped in Fletcher Henderson and the Swing Era, it was clear the musicians could play their asses off. They had such a big bold sound; they could do anything. One left a Sun Ra concert exhilarated.

What I learned from seeing Gil Evans and his orchestra, whom I caught a couple times as well in that same decade, was different. We won't worry about whatever perceived distinctions there may be between a big band and an orchestra, in jazz terms; doesn't matter. Like Sun Ra, by the '80s Gil Evans had had a long career. He had worked with many fine musicians over the years, and one of his chief talents—as was often said—was as a colorist, using his fellow bandmembers for their own special tone and personality, so that the varying and overlapping rosters each had their unique sound. I'm pretty sure I saw his band play at the New Morning and also at the grand Théâtre de la Ville; at least once George Lewis was in the lineup and Steve Lacy too. So, it was nice to be able to witness the organic particularity of his current orchestra, according to the people involved. Was Phil Woods also in the band one of those times? I think so. Always you could find musicians you knew from other contexts there to make up part of the Gil Evans palette.

There were others, of course, other big bands and large ensembles and orchestras, especially with lots of horns, that I had the privilege to enjoy in live performance. There was Luc Le Masne and his bright popping jazz orchestra Bekummernis, and earlier in the '80s the Vienna Art Orchestra, dazzling in their own way. Later that decade, there was Dizzy Gillespie with his all-star United Nation Orchestra that included Sam Rivers, pretty stupendous. And maybe the same year, an ensemble that was big on spectacle, effectively so, more prominent than the music itself, with masses of horns, and masks and costumes too: Urban Sax. I saw them as part of the Fête de la Musique, the evening of the summer solstice, on the sloping lawns of the Square Willette, the park leading up to Sacre Coeur. Clusters of horn players at various spots in close proximity, so that we all stood among them, as they kept honking out their quasi-minimalist patterns.

It strikes me that I probably saw more large ensembles during my decade in Paris than I have through all the years since in New York, but still there were some. The Mingus Big Band, down in the Time Café on Lafayette Street, with Ray Anderson on trombone and Ronnie Cuber on baritone. Would that be around the year 2000 or so? Mingus is always stimulating music, and many of his pieces are old favorites for me. As a legacy band, even with changing personnel, they do his music proud. And in more recent years—twice now, once down at SubCulture on Bleecker and last year at BAM—I've been impressed by Darcy James Argue's Secret Society, a big band of remarkable cohesiveness and depth, and clearly epic ambitions thematically. In that respect, the performance at BAM was almost too much for me, seeing how the work, *Real Enemies*, incorporated numerous video screens over the mise-en-scène of the big band all in pursuing a theme of conspiracy theories. And why not, I suppose, if you're gonna go big. Be that as it may, the majestic fullness of sound that one absorbs, physically and in spirit, attending a big band concert, really there's nothing like it.

Snow Crunch

Winter; snowy terrain. I walk along roads and paths careful not to slip on the ice. If I fell and hit my head, who would hear the dull thud, a muted and brief event? Like any blow to the body, louder from inside than out. So, I tend to keep toward the side of the road where the snow is still crusted, and the crunch underfoot, step after step, tells me that the treads on the soles of my shoes are gripping the ground and I will not fall. That is a sort of bluff, but which grants a certain security. At least while I remain alert for the sound. As I walk and gaze about through the trees, turning my head for a wider perspective, I soon forget to watch my steps, forget about the steady crunch of confirmation, and before long my foot goes sliding. So quiet that sliding, the whisper of ice, ice unsuspected. But I catch myself and remember what I know, seek out the passing crunch of certainty. Step after step my feet go biting into the ground, and the snow crunching in response says I will hold you.

MUSIC AND NUMBERS

What is *not* made of numbers? Skin, heart, bone. Love, touch, sex. Human languages, and all our many, many misunderstandings. Each person's notion of God or any other supreme force. The entirety of the vast non-human world. But music? From one end to the other, it is riddled with numbers: measures, frequencies, scales, octaves, harmonics; and almost every means of production. Almost? Must leave room for off the grid, for the unexpected, for spontaneous propositions of form. Yet does it sound like numbers? Certainly not. Numbers have no predetermined sound, no natural equivalencies, without a definition of terms. We would never suppose we were listening to numbers, but in the digital age the takeover is practically complete. Look under the hood, as it were, layers upon layers of numbers go pulsing about. Disturbing to think that the numbers are always there, though we cannot see them, flashing along through the realms of the immaterial—even more immaterial than sound itself. What will succeed the digital era? I cannot possibly imagine. A century ago, who imagined that sound information would be processed through digital means? Still, we hear a guitar, a voice—let's give it a rustic setting—no hint of numbers beyond the simple formalities of a musical system. With words or paint, we don't have to concede even that much. Patterns are not numbers exactly, nor is repetition, although the fixed metrics of traditional verse borrow the numerical to impose a standard. Traditional verse derives from oral practice, where the mind rigs its devices in order to remember. And mnemonics are often most easily reduced to numbers.

Words, though, seem the contrary of numbers, and perhaps a kind of antidote—even if we would be unable to grasp numbers, to wield them or be tripped up in turn, without words. By that I also mean the sound of words; not being music, or not being music yet, they stand their ground against numbers (until we are compelled to count them). Since verbal language is a translation of experience, as well as an experience in itself, words feel far less abstract than numbers; and words, every time they hop a fence, must be translated again, suggesting their meaning is only provisional. Indeed, beyond that fence, our words, the words we've always carried with us, when offered to others there, end up more abstract than numbers. In such circumstances, where the words are no longer familiar, where they've become strange and indecipherable sounds, they might as well be music, except they're not. They've lost the blood and breath underpinning them, without finding berth in the numerical superstructure we know as music.

The Parental Ear

When I was growing up in the 1960s and later through college, living at home, my sense of access to the parental ear was that it was a matter of hierarchy, birth order. As the baby in the family, at family dinners I was good for occasional amusement but don't overdo it; my turn in the spotlight was more like a kind of punctuation. That instinct for the position of punctuator—one foot outside, entering at various moments with a remark that might be clever and even possibly decisive—has remained with me ever since. My brother as firstborn and number one son had the serious seat, he was chief adept, the emissary abroad, groomed to follow in line, whether he wanted to or not; my sister, as only girl and middle child, was not just the princess with her own room but also second chief adept, dutiful, caring, and with a little luck, though no guarantees, obedient too; me, I was the extra, the wild card, far flung in mind and spirit, hardly willing to be contained. My antennae, therefore, were to be regarded with caution: who knew what manner of alien behavior I'd bring inside? Such was the structure, the prioritizing of listening when we all gathered, or so it seemed to me at least, and the family dinners continued once a week until I moved out and away after college.

Beyond the family dynamic, though, which often follows patterns laid down long before we were born, individual dialogues between parents and child are more open to negotiation, or so we endeavor to believe until the end. Through high school and college, it was just me and my parents in their house and I persisted in thinking I could tell them almost anything on my mind or about what I was up to. I have always been a sucker for honesty—and the straight face of others fools me nearly every time—though I also learned early on the value of discretion, albeit relegated to a secondary instinct. Indeed, ever since those years I have had a running debate with my sister as to what we could or could not say to our parents: I maintained they were adults, they could hear it; she said no, they could not. But that just reflects our own perspectives within the family, does it not, she as the daughter and thus thrice scrutinized, me as the extra who was permitted and did not hesitate to claim the most liberties. At any rate, it's clear they were listening. When, in my mid-teens, I would go on at the dinner table in expressing my opposition to the war in Vietnam, my father sometimes got very upset at my lack of respect for flag and country, grateful son of immigrants that he was (I don't recall him ever expressing to us what I suspect was his own opposition to the war). Around the same age, I asked my parents' permission the first time I slept with a girl since it was overnight at her house, or rather in a cottage in back of her house (this *was* Berkeley and environs early '70s): my father, speaking for both of them, replied that I could have said I was sleeping at Joe Schmoe's house, it was not a problem. Perhaps I should have been more gracious with my parents, but I thought that by talking to them I was sharing what I was living, and that they might want to know. Sheer self-indulgence on my part.

Many people don't want to hear about such things, I'm well aware, probably most people don't. I am the sort who sometimes skirts the edge, given a willing ear, of offering too much information, because I'm always a bit surprised people are listening to me at all—as if, still at the table, heads have turned my way at last and it all comes pouring out, the personal and impersonal tangled inextricably, scarcely time to edit, opinions and confessions and quotidian observations and half-remembered facts, who is listening anymore, as they slowly turn away again. It's not the sound of my own voice that enchants me, I'd rather hear others speak and take my place among them, sharing our discoveries together. To hold forth is fine if in the same spirit you listen, with a great big breath and arms open wide listen. The important thing is to open oneself, to talk, and to help others talk.

I have always encouraged my own children to talk to me, and to speak up when we were all together. Of course, there was never any likelihood that they would not. No built-in family hierarchy constrained them, just the clash of personalities sometimes. From the time they were small, I tried to speak of whatever I knew about the world, and to let them know that adults including myself, though probably not their mother, get a lot of things wrong. Being the more permissive parent, it may well be that they did not listen to me, as my wife liked to claim, yet I'm pretty sure they heard me nonetheless.

Breaking Things

Along a dirt road in the woods, over a series of ruts left by tire tracks through the mud, the ice that lay across them had a frosty cast, opaque as clouds, unlike the shiny sheets of ice on the ground nearby. I thought, it's below freezing outside, why not try? One careful step, then another triumphant, until I was marching slowly upon every rut, savoring the dull yet resonant sound of the cracking and crumbling. Half an inch thick, that skin of ice covered no water underneath, which must have drained into the cold dirt. So, back and forth I stepped, gleeful at the celebration of all that breaking. And what if someone hears my happy mayhem, I wondered briefly in passing. Who cares if they think I'm daft or acting like a child? But would I, should I share it with another, let them have a chance? Too late, not enough to go around; I was having too much fun to leave any unsmashed.

The brittle seasons bring their own abundant gifts for those of us inclined to partake of them. Among my earliest sensations, I think, was an inexplicable joy at the clattering, crackling, loud dissolution of autumn leaves. Wonderful to go leaping into a cool, cacophonous pile of leaves; better still to go stomping where they gather, kicking them against each other, send them flying, never to scatter quietly, with each pass the resonant breakage a little finer underfoot. In the Jardin des Plantes, in Paris, when I lived nearby in the early '80s, I would often go strolling up and down the long alleys of plane trees, my gaze aloft at the high canopy they formed, the birds gliding all the way just underneath, as I aimed deliberately for where the leaves had accumulated, to kick up a percussive snap and clatter just by walking through them. If someone ever invites me to their castle, and wonders at my absence in the hour of the feast, there they'll find me up some alley stomping through the heaps of fallen leaves.

But is it not, quite literally, the sound of breaking that grants such pleasure? When a glass or a window shatters, subtract concern or anger, is not our interest heightened, can we refrain from turning our head to look at the patterns that result, their fascinating singularity? Disaster movies, mere car wrecks, have long captivated audiences but cut out the sound and the sight is far less disturbing, less real; cut the image instead, and we see it anyway. And aren't the promises of revolution predicated on breaking, tear down the old institutions so we may build something new and somehow better, truer? We want to really hear the breaking, with its sensual and existential thrill, for it reminds us we're alive, that we're still here, survivors of our complacency, and from that destruction, that sound sprung from nothing, a space is formed where surely something else will come along.

ART AND FRIENDSHIP

The distance between a listener and a work is usually a matter of strangers in the night. With each visit, the work becomes a little more familiar; and with each work by the artist or composer that the listener has experienced, the more they will know the artist's sound world. But the distance remains to some degree one of strangers. What, then, when the listener and the artist meet, become friends, comrades? It may be the listener never heard a note before they met, or perhaps the music didn't register, or drew resistance. Knowing the person opens us to what they do, if we are well disposed toward them or simply curious; it fortifies our patience, suspends our instinct of rejection toward all we have convinced ourselves we don't need to know or wouldn't like anyway. We listen to one, and another, and another work by that friend, and rather than dismiss any of it we scratch our head and say instead that we prefer certain things more than others by that person. It all feeds the imaginative biography of the friend, the tone portrait of who they are, where they've been, and amplifies the mysterious happenstance of how we ever crossed paths with them.

But are we being too indulgent, just because we like the person? Is there some reflex of hypocrisy that emerges, where normally, if we'd come upon the same piece and it was by someone we knew nothing about, we'd change the channel before a minute was up? We must have been lucky, getting to know them informally: it grants us special entry, an opportunity to reframe and expand our attentions. By talking as friends, as to breach that distance of strangers forevermore (at least for a while), we become more than their audience. We accept that what they offer might not be what we thought we were looking for, but because it comes from them we want to hear it.

All-Consuming Noise

In one of Buñuel's late films, *The Discreet Charm of the Bourgeoisie*, there is a recurring motif where no sooner do some of the characters launch into a discussion, a plane overhead or a pneumatic drill out on the road or unexpected military exercises nearby drown out the dialogue. The joke is on us the viewers, though, since the characters go on talking to each other all the same. The sense of displacement that befalls us, as in a dream, only amuses us because we know—we hope—it is temporary. Were the irruption to persist throughout, separating what we hear entirely from what we see, the experience would sooner prove upsetting. Frustration would mount, anticipation would sour, and we would end up angry at the filmmaker for subjecting us to such madness and at ourselves for putting up with it.

That all-consuming noise, its examples multiplying the moment we think of them, stands as a challenge to our powers of concentration but also of distraction, and to our patience as well. In winter when the temperature inside dips below the thermostat setting and the furnace roars into action for a while, we notice and forget about it almost in the same instant, happy rather than bothered, reassured that we will stay warm. If we dwell on the sound at all, it is to find encouragement. No such solace accompanies the erratic ebb and flow of a vacuum cleaner nearby, except perhaps in that we are not the one doing the unpleasant labor, as the machine goes sucking up into its belly every manner of dust and dirt and crumbs. As it roots about, we do not ignore the noise so easily, regardless how quiet and expensive the model. Perhaps that is due to its steady irregularity, or the fact that someone else is doing the work while we are not, or the implicit threat of what we somehow recognize as the sucking sound and its absurd potential to grow suddenly monstrous. Meanwhile, the one who is doing the vacuuming may not actually mind it because they are getting paid for the tedious if not difficult work, or because they know they are getting the place clean, or because that noise emanating from the machine at the end of their arm provides a kind of cloud for their thoughts to go floating about, on an all too fleeting mental vacation.

The warmer months offer greater invasions, obviously, for we open our windows like an invitation. Noises from outside are thus louder and may by chance conspire, in abundance, to occupy the foreground, to crowd out any space for listening. But a fan, at close range and aimed directly at us, can be enough to commandeer every sound outside and also of our thoughts. What, then, of the air conditioner, all doors and windows shut, which grants us the perverse privilege of freezing in the heat and even quietly, across the room, emits that unmistakable shivering sound which reminds us, when we pause to notice, that we are sitting in a room-size, or house-size, refrigerator? Our habits might adjust, but it may well be that no other sound can enter from outside, not the knock on the door, the neighbor falling down the steps, nor even the airplane crashing into the house across the way.

But inside the plane, if it does not crash (though we know it always can), we are marinated in a noise that would seem to leave room for nothing else. And yet it's a porous sound, that tremendous white noise of the engines. Our hearing finds passage; we do not have to shout; and the baby in the seat behind, before it wears itself out from crying, manages to annoy us. As with electric cars—though there it's more the reverse dynamic, from outside, where the pedestrian does not hear its perilous approach—an altogether quiet engine would sooner panic us (even with the industry bragging endlessly, in that scenario, about the technological advances it has made). A plane *should* be noisy, that's another reason we know we're flying through the air; otherwise, we're falling. If we pay attention, at least intermittently, the great white noise can be a screen of many wonders: it filters out the world below; it lets us forget we were not born with wings; and even our waiting to arrive, which would seem to accelerate as we get closer, slows down instead and allows us to savor the going.

Music while Writing

Years ago, in a number of interviews I did with older writers, I tended to ask them at some point about music. Did they listen much? What were their preferences? How did it count for them? Inevitably I zeroed in on a question that especially interested me: did they listen to music while they wrote? Some replied never or not usually, a few admitted they sometimes did or remarked how that changed for them over time. Often, then and since, I remained on the lookout for that theme when reading comments from other writers. I thought even to make a survey, but let it go. Who would be interested in the question but me?

Has to do with divided attention—though maybe it's not really divided. It's about doing two things at once, yes, and stories abound where brain surgeons or master chefs or many a painter also have music playing while they work. So, why not word work? What makes thought and the articulation of language, the spinning out of verbal material and hammering it into shape like a shield or a road or a river, an activity that could be impeded by music more than any other enterprise would be? Properly speaking, when we listen to music, we shouldn't be doing anything else, unless perhaps we're dancing or simply walking. Nam June Paik, when I interviewed him, defined good music as something you could listen to with your eyes closed. We quickly get into definitions with such matters, distinguishing one kind of music from another and their respective places in our life. Music, if it could be asked, would prefer we surrender to it, knowing that sooner or later we will. And yet, mostly we listen to music in the background or as accompaniment while we do something else, even as company to not be so alone. Our attention, rather than divided, is augmented, our attention *span* is stretched, like a bridge that reaches further across the world than we'd imagined.

Another way to consider the play of our attention is to realize that it is not just one thing. Our attention is multiple: multivalent and multidirectional, splashing about in the simultaneity of experience. Just as we have five or more senses, and peripheral vision, and depth and breadth to our hearing, we also exercise a sort of secondary attention, and presumably more. We may not always be conscious of where our attention goes on our behalf, and surely it ventures against our will at times, but we needn't be afraid of where it takes us. Some people manage to train their attention to the point of performing marvels, very well for them; others are content, or merely helpless, to let it wander where it can, in the belief that it is naturally domesticated and will come home eventually. But bring music into the picture, and all bets are off. Seduction or healing force, its hold on our attention is hardly predictable.

In contrast to words and the thought it takes to digest them, music *seems* relatively easy to consume. Thus, the notion of background music, soundtracks, even furniture music; or, as mere goad to the physical. But *consume* is an odd word in speaking of music; is music a substance, a food? No question we can feel its effects on our system. So-called difficult music challenges our well-worn comforts; and a hint of the exotic may lift us out of what we thought we knew. In listening to music when I write, I have sometimes thought of it as choosing the mental landscape around me, some element of mood and coloring and energy, which may cover up as well the incidental sounds nearby. At any rate, let's just say, I have seldom chosen music that my childhood schoolmates would listen to. But like some older writers I spoke with long ago, I have found I put on music less and less while bouncing words around the caverns of my head. I cannot really say if the music helped or hindered the writing, probably both. Is it that the nature of my own listening has changed, along with my processes of thought and imagination?

Surely all that, and also something to do with aging, the evolving circuitry of my attention, the accumulation of experience, the synapses of memory lost or found, and let's not forget whatever my metabolism is up to. Since I have always approached writing as a form of listening in itself, perhaps the words have gotten louder, or more demanding, or just more squirrelly, leading me on and on before they're even written until I'm lost. Perhaps the music has also wised up, as to throttle me while saying, Enough with the two-timing already! And maybe that is what those older writers felt as well.

Whistling Fool

The time signature remains the same, that has never changed—my footsteps. If there was a time before the habit took hold of me, as there probably was, I cannot recall what it was like, that emptiness, or if not emptiness that waiting, that invitation, that gathering into forward motion just below the wellsprings of consciousness, because I am a fool for whistling. Whenever it started, and surely long before, meandering through the confused whisper of the world, that whistling tripped forth from the cranial jukebox and once let loose found perches near and far, in the most unsuspected corners, or else right in front of me, curious at my inattention until that moment. A friendly sound, untrained, not quite full-bodied and lacking a perfect tone, it doesn't care about the hearing or the airing or the faring, obstacles sooner give it strength, as it rises and floats, bouncing unbidden off hidden embankments or bending away to test intervals, chance ladders to climb and stepping off, vanish. The truth is, I don't know where it goes until it gets there, nor what stirs it awake exactly. Maybe someone said a word or mentioned a cultural reference, maybe the shape of a thought or the rhythms of light, branches, passing surfaces, the unintended sequence of a noise, a horn, a crack in the sky, produce an opening, the glimpse of an opening, and I fall in. If I was given a formula to plot its course, some kind of plan or algorithm, I would not know how to use it, and the whistling would wend its way regardless, ever unpredictable.

The melodies that unfold, I suppose, have to come from somewhere; or not. Someone's happy, I've been told, and yet I don't think happiness is especially the generator either. Every season and every mood provide their tones, their hints of a phrase or memory. Does the whistling anticipate my moves? Sometimes I'm certain that it does. Hey, let's try this, it says, and off we go. But even when a tune slips mysteriously into my thoughts, and I carry it along in my whistling, no matter how carefully I trace it, before long memory stumbles and lands me on a different note, what might seem a wrong note, which then leads to new paths and possibilities and I've lost the thread completely. But I can do that, who else but me, since I'm the whistling fool. Besides, if it sounds like a concert, that's only accidental. I have no responsibilities to an audience, nor to mastering an instrument, just pucker up my lips and blow. Can take it where I may, or let it take me, we'll get there together anyhow.

MATTER SPEAKS

Surely there is a sound life of objects and things just beyond us. What may seem silent to our ears might not necessarily be silent in another scale or frame of time. The warping of wood, the stretch and twist and bend of the material long after the branch has fallen or the tree has been cut, we are not likely to hear it; but that slow internal movement of the solid mass, that letting go down to the chemical level, does it not stir the air around it, set sound waves in motion even to a small degree? Would highly sensitive recording equipment, geared to the proper duration of that action, be able to capture the sound? Or, right at the center of the instrument, a piano sounding board, as it begins to crack from heat and dryness, that prolonged sound event can hardly be appreciated in itself except for the echo it pushes from the strings perhaps. The workings of organic matter, with their intricate dynamics, might well be considered for a proliferating alphabet of unsuspected sound properties, but what of simpler processes?

Yesterday, after washing a small cheap thermos and placing it upside down in the drainer, I noticed what I thought was the faint gurgling static of a radio signal nearby, as if it were about to tune in a message from afar. I couldn't for the life of me figure out where it was coming from, what pipe or appliance or conjunction of household elements might be producing it, as I leaned in to investigate. Then I looked at the thermos, turned it right side up, glanced at the slight bit of water in the bottom. I held it to my ear; sure enough, there was the source of the sound, though I still saw nothing that explained it. Today, same comedy, the thermos as innocent looking as ever.

Try as we might to ignore it, matter keeps speaking to us. In the constant wash of cars over a highway, from our stationary vantage point at a distance, what are we hearing? Friction. Less the velocity of engines moving through space, I think, the rubbing of rubber on macadam as the tires roll along resounds across the landscape, a reflection of our unsettlement. All things rub against each other, on other planets too, wherever there are elemental forces, a sun, an atmosphere. Our hands caressing our lover's body—are we listening to that? probably not—and I wonder, minus the dramatics of moans and whispers, minus the creaking of furniture, just the sounds of skin against skin, would we know? Would we hear it as our skin, and our lover's skin, and their singular meeting?

LISTENING AND THEATER

You go find your seat, probably not in the orchestra unless you've been lucky or had a good month, and probably not way up in the second balcony unless you just had to be there and don't mind peering far below toward the toy figures down on earth; you settle in, assess the measure of comfort and compromise, and you're ready. Let the talking begin. But there's always something to remind you it is not a pure event, an inevitable flaw that slightly mars the experience if you let it, a quirk of chance that may even pertain to your exact spot in the hall. Some people I know have a cosmic talent for ending up right in front of a long-legged lughead, or behind a tall person with big hair, or most often next to an habitué with an incessant need for lozenges who neglected to unwrap them beforehand, or who can't help whispering to their neighbor, or laughing or humming in an annoying manner and for too long; the intruder is quickly made aware of the disturbance they cause, so the terms are set. My own habit generally is to make do and rather to ignore the stupid little noises and fussiness of unconscious creatures. The strange paradox of live theater, after all, is that no matter how ritualized and rehearsed the performance, no matter how scripted, actors and spectators are still there in the present moment, all doing our best to stay focused on our collective transport to somewhere else. And as audience, we have a special task in that inadvertent compact: not only to forget ourselves and our neighbors, but to essentially freeze our body, render it silent of movement in order to effect the magic.

Among the many tenets of make believe that theater insists on, one shared by classical traditions and every stylistic approach since, and without which theater could hardly exist, is the orderliness of its dialogues. That may be so obvious as to not merit comment, but I have often been struck (even in the midst of such transports) by how characters listen to each other, and we with them, before the other responds. As if it were the most civilized tennis match. Sure, no dialogue is possible without that reciprocity, among a group as well, but offstage put more than four people together and the dialogue will splinter into two or more threads. That soon becomes confusing for the idle listener, and for some participants as well. Think of the person sitting at a dinner table, one conversation to the right, another to the left; as they engage in one, they catch snippets of the other, and thus intrigued contribute to that one as well. They don't entirely belong to either, and both groups know that, while the person continues to bounce between them, uncommitted or undecided. A clever writer may seek to portray a like situation before an audience, of simultaneous or intersecting conversations, but the device cannot be sustained for long; even then, it requires tricks of staging and carefully worked out rhythms to create the illusion of simultaneity.

So much can be achieved by the confluence of sight and sound in theater, but I have also noticed that to a large degree it doesn't matter where you're sitting to gain entry to the experience. Whether it's tiny figures way below or giants towering over us, their words, the tone and pacing of their speech, and the texture of their exchanges, reach us more or less the same regardless of distance, thanks to projection and acoustics or simply microphones. Far away, at least without opera glasses, we miss the finer nuances of facial expressions, but the gestures and movements of the actors in that shoebox, their positions through the space, make most everything clear. When they're too close in our face, we miss the balanced perspective, but still that does not quite hinder our enjoyment. Near or far, the images unfold before our eyes, but we are transported, I think, chiefly by the voices, which remain of equal size for all of us.

Music Plays

If we considered all the mental and physical processes at play when we are in the presence of music, the enormity of the machine inside might make us pause. We can relegate it to the background, just half-listen or not even, music still manages to get through to us on some level, finding entry through our distraction, through the passageways of dreams, in the pulse of our reflexes, no invitation necessary. In that respect, the ways we receive it beyond hearing, I wonder how a deaf person might feel music when in the vicinity, where the thump of percussion or amplified bass are not a feature. Are deaf people tuned more acutely that they might perceive it internally, like some marvelous contraption of minute tuning forks pitched in the blood and the nerves? I'm not talking about synesthesia here, which I have occasionally wished to experience, preferably with an off switch; nor the wiles of imagination either.

Surely the kind of music will affect our ability to hear it inside out, as it were. This is not merely a matter of genre or accessibility, but rather its special animation, the relationship of its sounds, how regular the pacing, the degree to which we may anticipate where its phrases go or its textures change. And since none of us have the same accumulation of sound experiences, nor the same network of cultural referents over time, we will in effect hear the same piece of music a little differently, and listen differently as well. No surprise there; were our perception exactly the same, that would be frightening. Even the tone of a single instrument finds its own way through each of us.

Deep within a performance itself, though, I wonder can a sharp listener discern whether the music generated in that moment is improvised? Will its effect on us be inherently any different? Will our distraction, or attention, seize upon it, draw it into us by the same channels as music that is composed, practiced, measured note for note? I suspect there is a substantial gray area of overlap where the cleverest listener would have difficulty thus identifying certain sections in music of a particular thrust and density. Does it matter, as we listen (perhaps despite ourselves), whether the note or cluster or sequence unfolding was intended to be right there or if they fell into place only in present time? Music plays us either way. We are its instrument.

OLD FOLKS

I have always had a certain reverence for old people. As a child, that meant my grandparents, their friends and relatives; at the *shul* we went to in Asbury Park, that also meant someone like Zimmel Resnick, who my father once told me ran guns for Israel before it was a state (which sounded like ancient history to me, though it was all of twenty years prior). Every one of them had come from somewhere far away, across an ocean and then some, long ago. What could I possibly ask them, as a boy of suburban comforts who knew almost nothing and had no idea of such journeys? How did you ever find your way? Nor did it occur to me to ask. I don't recall my grandparents once mentioning their lives back there; those places did not exist anymore, you couldn't go if you wanted to and who would want to? Even so, it surprises me today to think I didn't wonder much about those unknown lands. What stories my grandparents offered were parenthetical and pertained only to the present or the recent past.

Later, in my teenage years, I lived closer to my maternal grandparents and visited a bit more often, yet it did not enter my head to view them as living history, resources to explore. Or perhaps for a college paper, nothing further.

Somehow I hardly understood the value of what they might tell—not anything famous, just life—I was looking elsewhere, beyond, not in front of me. After college, living in LA for a year in the late '70s, I was friends with a woman my grandmother's age, a Russian-born former actress, Elena Miramova Moore. When she married Captain Moore in the mid-1940s, she left her acting behind, but she had known fame and success in her day. I encouraged her stories on my visits, but never attempted any formal interview, and all I remember (besides that she wrote the play *Dark Eyes*) is that she had played the lead in *Saint Joan* in London and had been friends there with Vivien Leigh. I asked if Shaw had seen her performance: "Why, he took me to the theatre!" she replied. Problem is, when I glance on the internet now to refresh possible details in my mind, I find no mention of her in the London production of the play, only in Berkeley in the '40s. Could be I misheard. Plus, I've just learned two other details that I wished I knew back then: she went to Berkeley High School some fifty years before I did, and in the late '40s she was a regular visitor to the home of the great Icelandic novelist Halldór Laxness—whom I only discovered 25 years after I knew her. So much for listening, I suppose, when you're too young to know what to listen for.

But somewhere along the line, I began to develop the

idealized notion, based on fleeting encounters with one and another old person, each fascinating in their singular way, that someone should really get down each person's story, should listen to them and ask questions before it's too late. Not that I imagined it would really happen in most cases, or that there was any proper repository for such harvests besides a shoebox in a closet or a dusty library shelf. And when I see the depth of resources available online now, the vast untold quantities of nearly forgotten books and documents and audio and video recordings, as can be found plunging through one site alone, the Internet Archive, and extrapolating from there, I shudder at the infinite prospects of such collections. Which means, by implication, that any individual story, no matter how personally momentous, would seem to shrink in significance among the multitudes. And yet, it does not. There is almost always someone who remembers, or discovers again, or recalls having heard from someone else. That significance is never lost entirely, in a local sense at least, the story of where one has been.

Now that I myself am a bit older, in late middle age, do I still entertain that idealized notion? I think it would be wonderful for every old person to have the opportunity to tell their story, to have it taken down for after they're gone, to grant them one last chance to send a message in a bottle to the future; and for their voice to be recorded, that it might still be heard. Aside from matters related to storage of that wealth, however, other complications come into play. On one end, the listener, who is also the questioner and documentarian: probably that person should not be too young, mid or late twenties minimum; they must be patient but unafraid and have a sense of why they are listening, especially if the subject has led what would seem an ordinary life. Then there is the enterprise itself: I keep referring to the old person's story, where in reality we're all aware that one life holds many stories at once, which are not necessarily coherent in their totality just because one has lived them; so, how long should the telling be, shall some kind of limit be imposed? The greatest paradox, naturally, is the subject, the old person in question, the carrier of these riches. First, what constitutes "old"? I would think eighty at a minimum, that sounds verifiably old, as if a person should be applauded for having made it that far. But life expectancy is a tricky thing in many communities and many families, some people are just not lucky in their health or birth or work or environment, and are clearly old at sixty. The criterion of age must therefore be flexible. The question brings with it an additional challenge: how to assess when it is not yet too late to talk to that person for the purpose of one or several interviews. The Bureau of Life Stories will no doubt need to allocate its resources carefully, thus the effort to keep more or less on schedule, so that volunteers and equipment remain available. And yet, despite all such preparations, the beloved (or not) old person may have another trick to throw down. All very well to be honored and recognized for achieving old age, and as if in reward sought out to be heard once more, but that oldster may well want none of it, not to play along and be pestered with questions, nor to build their own tombstone with life stories. They may not want to remember or be reminded, for the pain it brings back, the confusion, and the echo of all the little indignities that have only grown louder, not softer. The cheerful if reticent young interviewer may arrive ready to listen with all their heart, but the oldster just can't find the desire to cooperate, to demonstrate gratitude with the indulgence of a response, and instead breaks down weeping, then the young interviewer can't help weeping too and off they go, the stormy oceans, until finally—though final is surely the wrong word here—one of them asks the other, How about lunch?

HEARING THINGS

A saxophonist friend, Etienne Brunet, has written eloquently, angrily, imaginatively about the tinnitus that has afflicted him in one ear for some time. If we step into a café, half the time he walks right back out: even at a medium volume, the din is too painful. A low-level ringing is constant, and often a sort of static settles in that comes and goes without resolution. In the first years, he thought he was going to lose his mind, sank into a depression, consulted one doctor after another, each offering a different assessment of the problem; finally, at one clinic, a doctor told him if he'd come there at the start they could have repaired the damage, now it was too late. That was enough to drive a person over the edge, but somehow he has managed to keep going, his sense of humor intact or perhaps more finely sharpened. And, he is still creating new music! Sure, what else is he going to do, if that is what he does, but I am certain a listener would not hear the difference in his playing, no noticeable trace of the interference running through his head in the intrepid sounds he's producing. Oliver Sacks and others tell of rare cases where tinnitus causes the sufferer to even hear music. Cue the ice-skating soundtrack, or just a recurring phrase—what horror. How would a musician escape that? How listen past the cage of that melodic fragment, how domesticate it, how find rest?

But one doesn't have to get clinical to be hearing things. Some people I know insist they're bothered by the noises of a neighbor through the walls or out on the street, and when they look to me I'm embarrassed at the sudden lack of sensitivity in my hearing—maybe I'm not sitting in the right spot, or I was listening to something else—or because I think they've lost it and dare not say so. Of course, when the opposite occurs and I'm the only one who hears the curious sound, I know they're just not trying. Is it proof that something is there only when everyone hears it? Much as we may have mental and emotional blind spots, do we each have sonic blind spots as well? And shouldn't we treat the one who hears things, voices and other phenomena, with the same cautious respect as those who have visions? I mean, if they're not already crazy.

CONCERTGOING 10:
SENYAWA

The latest concert, two nights ago. What, even, to call the music? If that matters. It wasn't jazz, or punk, or traditional music. And yet, more than threads of all these in what the two Indonesian musicians of the band Senyawa were doing. I'd never heard of them until last month when my friend Michael in Brisbane, Australia sent me something about the group in an email. He had noticed they were going to play in New York—their first concert here, the singer told the audience late in their set—the other night at the Bridget Donahue gallery down on Bowery below Grand. I'd never been there, and the only information online, besides the address, was the names of the two bands and a link for buying tickets; which I did, not expensive, just for me. I had listened to some of their music online at the Free Music Archive and was intrigued by the musical space they seemed to be coming from: ardent experimentalists out of a strong traditional culture. Granted, Indonesia is a very big country and most of what I'd heard was gamelan music, while they had nothing of a gamelan sound, except perhaps obliquely in the rhythmic attack sometimes and in the sole instrumentalist's sound palette, above all because his instrument had a regional tonality, made of bamboo. Michael did warn me they can get pretty loud and also that I might not like them, which wasn't a problem.

The whole adventure, for me, was against the odds. With the current heat wave and high humidity, I do not venture out much. As mentioned, I do not go to hear music in Manhattan very often, when I've got so many choices in Brooklyn (and that's without even going as far as Williamsburg, which is a similar distance as lower Manhattan from where I live). Compounded with those factors was the discovery that the other group, the two-woman band I. U. D., was of a punkish bent—I never much cared for punk rock. So, why was I going? Why was I bothering to take the subway four stops on a hot steamy night just to be uncomfortable at the other end? Stubbornness, musical curiosity, the challenge of obstacles, who knows. Because I didn't know anything about the seating, or whether the place would be crowded, and because the reliability of the subway can be quite unpredictable (at night, in summer), I left the house an hour before the scheduled start of the concert. But since the train came within minutes, I arrived at the gallery exceedingly early, at 7:30. The tall young fellow by the door handed me my wristband, and when I uselessly remarked there were no chairs, he chirped it's punk, it'll be hot. As if to further induce an internal grimace, seeing how bare the space looked I asked if there had been much response. Oh yeah, he said, it's going to be full. The gallery was an empty loft, one flight up, what looked like the entire floor, probably 1,500 square feet at least. He also told me that I. U. D. was going first and starting a bit late.

Would I last? Every few minutes I reminded myself I could leave anytime. I dreaded the prospect of music that was painfully loud and hardly seemed like music while being surrounded by a crowd dancing like out of a mental ward. But the few people hanging about in back or up front hardly looked the part, and the band setup in the stage area was two electric drum kits with some electronics boxes in between plus two mikes and flanked by two midsize speakers. Nothing I couldn't endure for a couple of hours, I hoped. Halfway toward the stage I sat on the floor against the wall and busied myself with copyediting work for the next forty minutes, finishing shortly before the music began, as the audience trickled in and gradually filled the entire space, about two hundred people. I kept telling myself I could leave after the editing was done, just mosey on out as if I were going to smoke a cigarette—but I stayed right where I was in what had become a precious spot, my perch against the wall. I noticed possibly two or three people my age, but most were not much past half that, in their twenties and thirties. And then at last the din of the crowd subsided and the concert started.

From about where I was seated and right up to the stage area, everyone sat on the floor; behind me, a mass of people stood all the way back to the door. At any lull in the music, the din from the back of the crowd continued unabated, which I didn't understand. What were all these people doing here, I wondered, and who did they come to see? How did they know about the event? Was it because Senyawa had played at the WFMU studio in Jersey City the night before? Since when were Indonesian experimental musicians the cool thing to come out for here? Or was I. U. D. some kind of underground sensation? I wouldn't know from the music. The two women banged on their electric drum pads with varying degrees of enthusiasm, but they did reach a genuine thrashing intensity, and that along with the singer's extended screaming of words I couldn't fathom convinced me of their quasi-punk credentials, but I really didn't know what that meant now in music other than an esthetic choice (echoed by the T-shirt displayed on a rack onstage, with a crude drawing of a face and written under it the words Bad Sex). The electronics boxes did I don't know what, something, not really noteworthy, and there was also some looping in the vocal, that was fun for a moment. The singer often used both mikes—maybe one had the looping—and between getting worked up and banging on the drums, her headscarf soon unraveled and her long hair got loose. Mercifully, nobody started dancing in that tight space, nor standing in front of me either, and the band was kind enough to end their set in little more than half an hour. Finding myself still there in the spot against the wall where I first sat down, I knew I wasn't going anywhere. Even if the air felt too close, and the din of everyone talking again was oppressive, the band I came to see was about to go on. The drum kits and consoles were removed from the scene; only the mikes remained.

Without fanfare, the two musicians of Senyawa came out. The singer, a bandana over his head, appeared to be wearing an open leather jacket over his bare chest. The instrumentalist, long dark hair, was wearing a WFMU T-shirt I recognized because I bought one in the last fundraising drive. His instrument was an ongoing puzzle to me, since it looked like a valiha from Madagascar, way at the opposite end of the Indian Ocean seven thousand miles away. Over a length of bamboo, its strings were strung like a harp rolled up on itself, except this instrument was electric and most of the time he didn't play it quite like a valiha. If it was an Indonesian instrument, I do not know what a traditional approach would be. This gentleman did indeed pluck the strings sometimes, with all his fingers, but more often he strummed furiously with a pick, or else bowed the strings, which could build a nice wall of sound. He too made use of a looping device occasionally. The singer, agile and expressive, often gestured as he sang, arms hunched up like a monkey, stalking his song like a rock star. He could really wail when he wanted, or reach the low guttural sounds of throat singers, and then suddenly he was up in the soprano register with the most delicate of lines. So, some punkishness flashed in and out of their music as well, while I also thought intermittently of Phil Minton with his vocal acrobatics often improvised, as this singer really commanded an incredible range. You could see the sweat glistening on his skin. There were a lot of heads nodding along to the sympathetic wildness of the duo, and I wondered if, shall we say, most of the crowd had ever heard such sounds in their life. For my own account, I could not tell in listening how much had been worked out and how much was freely improvised. If their pieces were based in song form, I could make no sense of it. After three-quarters of an hour their music had increased its mystery for me, and feeling my mission for the night fulfilled I got up before they started what was likely their last piece and threaded my way out through the thick crowd to the slightly cooler air on Bowery as I made my way down to Canal Street and over to the Q train.

Simultaneous Translator

I don't know how they do it. Well, I do, sort of, I've done it myself, but if you stop to think really how it's done—no time for that, just open the faucet, the faucet of language—you go tripping all over yourself. Don't look down, it's a long way to fall, and for goodness sake don't go looking at the audience. You can't let your mind wander either or get snagged on a word. The only thing that's required of you is to listen, that's all.

Imagine if high-level international conferences—peace settlements, arms control, border disputes—decided to skip the human element and trust new technology to do automatic interpreting. Your kingdom for a cheese sandwich. Swords into timeshares. And who sent you, oh noble toilet cleaner? No one to blame when all goes wrong! The stress that those live interpreters and simultaneous translators must endure. I have known people who did such jobs at the UN and at immigration courts, though I never asked them much about the work. Off duty, they seemed as calm as anyone else in New York or Paris. I have only been tested twice in that way, at literary events—no high stakes but for the elegant setting. Many years earlier, I had been asked to interpret for a French interview with

Woody Allen, which I was nearly certain I could have managed, except I turned them down: I didn't want to blow it. Might have been smarter had I accepted.

The literary events, though, one was with Peruvian writers, the other with Argentine. It paid well, plus a nice dinner, why not. There were three Peruvians that night, I figured how difficult could it be, having never actually done live interpreting before. They talk, then I talk, we take turns. Or I should say: they talk while I listen, in the hope that my comprehension of Spanish will be up to the task. I discovered two things, at least. One of the writers tended to speak in paragraphs, whether reading his work or answering questions. I had neglected the wild card of memory in all this. Every so often he recalled that there was an interpreter at the table, and then he'd look at me. I was listening, and listening, and trying to keep listening, with the growing awareness that I could not possibly remember it all, not panicking but a little anxious just the same. Interpreting thus turned into an improvised mixture of conveying his words in translation and summarizing them. With each volley, I would smile and take a deep breath, the audience smiling with me, before I launched into whatever I could retrieve of the sequence, without second thoughts, hellbent on not leaving out anything important while eager to just get through it.

The other thing I noticed that night was how listening, or my own listening, doesn't always like to play along; it lingers, sniffs about, sends the mind bouncing across the universe—or a lifetime—in an instant. Attentively as I listened, even with the most helpfully paced reader a word or phrase would sometimes catch my thoughts, like ripples in a stream, before I hauled my attention back on track. When my turn came again, I was usually able somehow to glide over the slight gap in what I'd heard. The translator is used to having a near-invisible role, but was anyone in the audience watching me as I listened? Could they guess, by looking at my face, at the trips and traps I was running through?

Some time later, I attended another event presented by the same organization, dedicated to one of my favorite writers, a Brazilian who died many years ago. Though my Portuguese is rusty and was never fluent, I listened to the speakers and the translator, aware at various points where she got details wrong or left things out. I was a little pleased with myself that I could hear those discrepancies, despite my less than full mastery of the language, and wondered if she wasn't quite up to the job. A season or several after that, I played the interpreter again there at an evening that celebrated a series of new translations and anthologies of an iconic Argentine writer. My presence seemed hardly necessary, as two of the three speakers were longtime American professors and literary translators who had been in the business for forty years, but the famous personage who had been close to the writer apparently insisted on having an interpreter. The event rolled along easily enough, though at a couple spots where I hesitated in my translation, one of the professor-translators jumped in, in a friendly if slightly impatient way, to finish my sentences. When the famous personage unexpectedly pulled out a prepared text and I listened to her, I recognized what she was reading and thought this is ridiculous, she didn't need me here. Rather than get interrupted again in my efforts to translate, I reached into my bag for one of the anthologies that bore the same text in English as introduction. Whatever the audience may have thought of my performance that night, I was not going to work any harder than I had to.

What You're Asking

Who would be the most difficult interview you could do? The person closest to you. Why do you ask me that only now, she will say. Had you but known. You have a good idea what you could never ask, and do not try, knowing no response will be forthcoming. But of course, you could be wrong. Where you're certain of the answer that you'll get, you do not bother with the question. What would be the point? You ask because you want to know, so what is it that you don't know? Perhaps you'll have to ask yourself. Does it turn out that she is more familiar than you thought? Listen, she is speaking, can you hear? But it's just as you imagined, you know those words. She keeps telling you and telling you, and you think you're listening, except the words are something else. She will not tell you what you'd like to know but you could ask. Where would it take you if you did, that you should have to ask, and would you figure out what's next? It may well be that you are strangers, after all. You might have to keep asking her questions, you're bound to get it right; unless you don't. You know she doesn't like questions. Will she hear what you're asking? Just because you are so close does not mean she agrees to be questioned. No doubt she should be asking you instead. If she wanted to. It's all so difficult, the talking and listening, talking and not listening, asking and waiting, not talking and listening. Haven't you both heard it all before? Listen again.

Semana Santa, Sevilla

Not the exact words but the tone and the purpose I recall, Sevilla 1985, Semana Santa. Memory simplifies, leaves out heaps of ornate details, the large crosses, the brass bands, the baroque pageantry, doesn't matter. Two steps to the left! Forward, forward, forward. One step to the right! Forward, forward. The long processions with their white penitents' robes, another group in purple, another in gold or blue or red, some sixty such groups throughout the week, each took their turn according to an intricate schedule winding their way along the streets of the city, starting from their parish church to go all the way to the center of town, in through one great door of the grand cathedral and out another, then back along a different route to their parish church. The full circuit could take the better part of a day and by mid-week the processions were going around the clock. Some groups counted many hundreds of *procesionistas* all in their robes and conical hoods of matching or different color, and for an American who had only seen pictures of those robes in quite a different context, the echo was chilling. But here that image of pure American evil was blasted away before the magnitude of the practice, a four-hundred-year-old tradition perpetuated by the church faithful. Near the head of each procession were usually two elaborate platforms or parade floats, one bearing a statue of Jesus in one of the Stations of the Cross, and the other a statue of the Virgin Mary. Those imposing sculptures, lent by the parish church, might be centuries old or of more recent vintage; I don't know how they moved it onto the traveling platform, but the floats were each carried by twenty or thirty men—hidden underneath except when they took a rest—bent over with the padded crossbeams upon their shoulders, their lower backs girded by the thick, wide leather belts worn by furniture movers. Given their position, privileged though it was, the carriers could not see where they were going, and so it was the role of the *capataz*, the fellow in front, to call out loudly enough for them to hear the direction of each step they had to take. This was crucial at every bend along their route, where sideways or forward steps were measured and adjusted according to the angle. But the most impressive feat in those terms was on entering and, after a break, exiting the grand cathedral, for the floats did not seem to clear the wide doorways by very much. Precision, precision was clearly of the essence, and yet an improvised measuring on the spot.

¡Dos pasos a la izquierda! Adelante, adelante, adelante.

¡Un paso a la derecha! Adelante, adelante. If I close my eyes, I feel I can still hear them somewhere, thirty-plus years later. The heavy tread of the carriers, with all that is riding upon them. The meticulous calls of the front man measuring out their journey. The solemn steps of the many, many marchers behind them, on and on, the steady whisper of their linen robes as the material rubs against itself in forward motion, like there might be no end to them. The excitement of the crowd, not silent at all yet still hushed as witnesses. And do I hear a voice singing from some balcony, a lament older than Spain itself.

CROSS-DISCIPLINE SUSTENANCE

The theme of cross-discipline sustenance has long fascinated me. I know a photographer who draws much of her inspiration from poetry. One friend, an abstract painter I first met twenty-five years ago by way of a mutual friend, a musician, derives far more of his painting energy from music and musicians than anything else. Our musician friend, I have discussed books with him often, as I used to do with another musician friend, a prominent jazz saxophonist who was a voracious reader. But the non-musician music heads are a special breed, I suppose. That inexhaustible enthusiasm, for many kinds of music, I have shared as well with others who cultivate their gardens mostly outside the realms of art, though clearly graced with a wide curiosity: one friend who lives down the street, a lawyer, we have attended many concerts together; another, a political scientist who lives halfway across the planet from me, we have sent each other countless digital recordings through the internet, discoveries old and new.

My old friend Norton Wisdom, a painter I have known for more than forty years, takes his love of music further still. Though he remains dedicated to the obsessive and resourceful abstract format he developed long ago, music literally moved him out of the studio and onto the public stage where, since the beginning of the 1980s, he began to elaborate a parallel path that is mostly quite different, a sort of figurative expressionism style. Listening harnessed live music as the force that animates the hand holding the brush or other implements—a scraper, a sponge, a rag—and he often does not hesitate to apply his fingers directly to the paint for the sake of details like a flowing mane. He started his live painting in the punk clubs and dive bars of LA, and has performed in galleries and concert halls, amphitheaters and churches, on four or five continents and in the dodgiest watering holes in the middle of America, with musicians in jazz, rock, classical, funk, free improvisation, and beyond. He may not have imagined such reaches at first, but this too was how the music animated him, in that it took him out and further out of the art world, beyond a "proper" artist's career, beyond critics' presumptions and art school résumés, to a place where none of that much mattered. Indeed, his abundant activity as a performance painter has tended to cast a shadow over his studio practice in the eyes of professional arbiters. It was music that did this to him. After all, he always returned to the studio; he spent most of his time there. But the stage proposed a special risk that was more in the moment, as the music unfolded. That whole way of working caused him to adapt his methods and materials accordingly, until he had his setup worked out to the essentials. Instead of a canvas, he employed a backlit translucent panel that could be rolled up into a tube for travel. The water-based paints, which he could buy anywhere, allowed him to wash the work clean once or twice in the course of a performance, or even just partially, to take the morphing figures in another direction. Periodically during the evening, he would pause and step back to shoot a few digital shots of what he had done. But at the end of the set there was only an empty canvas, the painting as ephemeral as the music, nothing left but the documents.

Listening and Water

All it is is water. And somehow we always recognize the sound, though we hear it differently every time. Nothing to hold onto, like light slipping through our fingers. No sound is as sure an inducement to reverie, especially falling water in all its forms—water dropping from the sky onto the skulls of the thirsty. In the shower inevitably I space out, it happens in an instant, my mind goes who knows elsewhere. I get ideas, I connect things, my thoughts percolate and pop while the spray falls steadily upon my head, my back, my arms. At moments I forget about water or where I am. The sound is a curtain, a carpet, a screen for transports. I don't even recall what brought me there. It can't be helped, some sort of magic stirs about when we step into the shower.

Those spontaneous leaps of mind, those mindsprings, are not just a phenomenon of standing naked under the shower, immersed in its sound and its tactile embrace. Like a personal theater, that indoor space where the downpour is well regulated would seem to favor wayward thoughts. But rain, in all its irregular majesty, comes drumming down around us upon countless mute surfaces, sounding them afresh. If we are not too put out by the deluge we may be transported, as though we were walking through a music brought out by the rain. Nicest is to skip the discomforts altogether, pull up a seat by the window and attend the concert. Except, where everything becomes a sounding board to the drops upon drops of inexhaustible rain, the best listening will be had of course somewhere out in the middle of it. Only serious listeners need apply.

In that regard, I wonder—this must exist somewhere—if in some rainy clime a serious listener ever took the trouble to build a home that maximized its sounding properties when the rain came down, by the use of different materials (wood, skin, glass, metal) and fashioning various kinds of hollows and triggers, so that the drops could play the entire dwelling. Or maybe it would be wiser, in that madness, just to construct a room or a cottage for such purposes, in order to also be able to escape the musical house.

But to follow a certain train of thought (off its unfinished tracks), if water is coming down and it's not rain, and you're not in the shower, then it must be snow. Which leads me to speculate, in the spirit of useless inventions: why aren't homes equipped with an attachment to the shower head from which snow might fall? Could be a little cold standing there naked, but more importantly, what would it sound like? Clearly, that is the province of the careful listener, for the drumming of snow is no drumming at all but the lightest touch, as if gravity were an afterthought. On the porch, eyes closed, we might hardly hear the snow falling outside. Thip thip thip; or not even; th th th. That sound at the threshold of hearing, like faint steps, takes us into its distant presence. We hear something is there—but it couldn't be quieter, or further away. When we look to see the fat flakes floating earthward, the sight drowning out the sound, we have to listen harder, each flake carrying its parcel of silence. Yet how can that be water too?

If water is indeed a sound-making substance—as we know it is and have experienced in many settings—its capacity for waves and sloshing about, or rushing headlong, or trickling in a stream, seems bound to haul us in its wake when we are near enough to hear it. The contours of its rambling or driven song become subtly our own, a rhythm to draw from, as if on some level we adapt to the breathing of a greater force. Reflex of our ancient thirst, we listen for water in all its guises. That voice, ever changing, is but the sound of its movement over resonant bodies. Earth's bow. How often we are led to thinking we hear water somewhere, but when we do it seeps into our consciousness, folds its voice deep within our ear. It tugs at our dreams, our terrors too; enchants us or puts us to sleep with its quiet amusements.

The quiet, after all, is water's gift. Distracted by its vocalizing, we forget how water sculpts away at the quiet, constantly marking it off—there, outside these restless burblings, is quiet all around. Like the edges of a pond or lake that lap the shore lazily, poetic reminder of the reigning quiet: because we can hear the water's shy movements, the edges lapping, we know how much quiet we are blessed with in that moment. Water, even at a roar, provides an accountability of the quiet. Beyond its sonic reaches, we are left in awe at the quiet that still exists and seems ever just the other side of the water, which may well comfort us as much as haunt us.

Anonymous

To be part of the audience at a performance or event is a curious practice. Where did we learn how to do that, to sit and listen and watch as a group? Children from an early age take to it quite naturally, though a bit of training along with a basic sense of etiquette is helpful. We are predisposed to listening; whether we maintain focus is another matter. But as members of the audience, we cast our consciousness outward toward the singular event that unites us for a while, in our club of strangers, as the self withdraws discreetly to the shadows. The occasion renders us nearly anonymous. We offer our presence at the event, our name has no bearing on the matter. And yet, why are we there? Each of us chose to go, to make the effort of going, each on our own. Like everyone else, we want to see what happens; and we want to remember it almost before it's happened.

A circuitous way to say that I often opt to go alone when I go to concerts. Not always; I do act sociable sometimes. But the reason I'm going is to hear the music. The places I frequent don't have reserved seats, and I have my preferences where to park myself. Besides, being sociable also means concern for the other person's enjoyment—

does she like it? is he getting bored?—and when that's a problem going to the concert becomes something else, more complicated. Put another way, I'm not trying to make any converts nor to win friends, but if someone wants to take a chance and join me, by all means, come along. In spite of what I might anticipate, the anonymity of the audience remains intact even if friends are there, for we each encounter the music in our own way, unknown to the others.

MUSICIANS

But who are these creatures and what are they doing here? More to the point, how do they listen to each other? It is not like doing anything else. Playing music together is a practice in simultaneity, listening while one continues to play. In most genres, where the work is more or less written, that instant feedback loop helps keep everyone directed toward the music they were intending to make. But in improvised music, notably free improvised music—thriving more than ever despite its often-announced demise over the past fifty years—this dynamic takes on a far more dramatic cast, for the music is unfolding in the moment, unknown to all concerned until it materializes before their ears. I am speaking especially of groups where there is no clear leader to follow, where the collective nature of the enterprise articulates an esthetic born of the occasion, but also of works that though they may be composed up to a certain point revel in indeterminacy to provoke a different music with every performance, whether via graphic scores or other devices that dispense with fixed notation. In all of these, the musicians listen their way forward, sensing the thrust or momentum of the music they are part of like a living organism, both carrying it along and being carried in turn. And it is by this listening from inside the moving present moment, alert to the gestures that they and their fellows are engaged in, that they may engineer a shift in direction toward unexpected openings discovered on the spot.

If that were not enough of a challenge, the foremost task for musicians in the midst of all else is to listen to oneself. Just as we must listen to what we are saying in the very act of speaking, in order to remain coherent (we hope), musicians have to maintain awareness not only of the sounds they are putting forth right now, but also where they are going with it and where they've just been; any repetition, for instance, should be conscious and purposeful, not the product of laziness or neglect. This all goes without saying, no doubt, and yet one must also leave room for the fruits of distraction, the felicitous accident, the better to capitalize on such gifts. In other words, consciousness need not be a restraint, nor inhibiting, but rather a kind of training, preparation for a certain porousness, to recognize the unforeseen. From our seats it may not seem the musicians are quite so absorbed, but there are worlds coming into existence that depend on their listening.

Language Loops

I admit to being an amateur in these waters, scuttling about in my three or four tongues with only one learned as a child, but I am often amused by the secret echoes that bubble up in the back and forth between languages. In the right conditions they can reveal clues about one culture and another, although the ear in its caprices may not always prove reliable.

The Iranian restaurant owner Manijeh is speaking to her Afghan employee in Farsi. She explains to us that he is actually speaking Dari, the Afghan tongue, but that to her it sounds like written Farsi of times past—she says it's a strange feeling and compares it to hearing the French of Molière spoken! From an American perspective, that's rather astounding. I wonder, wouldn't that make it difficult to listen to a person, to maintain a conversation?

Many years ago, early in my courtship of a certain French girlfriend, I'd noticed the tall voluminous curtain billowing up in her bedroom where it hung above the radiator. She commented affectionately, Yes, it's like a *montgolfière*. That proud Mongol became our mascot for a while, more than the hot-air balloon which the word actually meant. In the enchantment of those autumn months—stupid as our little joke was, born from my misunderstanding—our Mongol friend watched over us. That we took a foolish turn was not the Mongol's fault. A *personnage*, created from mistaken words, had gained spirit of a sort. In sympathy with us, we thought.

The ear may be a fickle organ, but it cannot pretend for long. The very pronunciation of a syllable may make a difference, bringing with it unwanted connotations, a bad taste. We hear these nuances sometimes when we meet people, but Ali tells me that, common as his name is in the Muslim world, when he hears it pronounced by Algerian Arabs, the drawn-out double-Ah they begin his name with sets him on edge, it all sounds much too rough. *Doucement*, he wants to say to them.

Silent Steps

Almost too quiet. As if the house were holding its breath. No tick or tock of old wood, no ricochet of bird song. The ear lifted up to the air just then, to find every thing lost in thought.

But for the faint creak of the floor. And again. Prowling through the rooms, footsteps unsounding, once in a while the cat presses a squeak from the boards. Here I was a moment ago, the animal says to the house.

I don't know where he is. Now that I'm listening for his slightest traces, I don't hear the fire engine sirens off in the distance, or the busy warblers nearby newly awoken. I'm convinced I can distinguish the hush of fur brushing past furniture, the intensity of the waiting, the stalking. Though no cat to be seen.

Concertgoing 11:
Audience of One

One night last month I went to a new house concert series in my neighborhood, and ended up after all these years having a new experience. Sooner or later, it had to happen: I was the only member of the audience; the audience was me. The situation was explained in part by certain mitigating factors, but still it was a little disconcerting to be the only person clapping after each piece. There was a duo playing, all improvised, woodwinds and strings; more specifically, bass clarinet, clarinet, shakuhachi alongside guitar or bouzouki. The reed player I knew a bit, around my age, played all over the world; his email blast was how I learned of the event. The guitarist lived there, barely, having rented the apartment only recently because of its proximity to Downstate Hospital where he had been appointed head of the psychiatry department. His wife and teenage kids had not yet moved from DC, so he gathered two sofas and an armchair in rows for the performance. I don't know how he had spread the word, but a geneticist friend of his showed up for the final piece, having gotten lost along the way. I was additionally curious because I had never met anyone who lived on that broad avenue which I knew solely as my closest route for driving to JFK airport, a road that always had traffic and plenty of double-parked cars. This was the first night of presenting music there, and he had apparently scheduled another such evening a week or so later. They played for an hour. The two instruments blended well in that small living room, like ivy over the bare walls. Sitting there as the person they were playing for, in a sense, I recognized my responsibility. For once, the luxury of anonymity was not an option. To the two musicians facing me, my role was integral to the equation. As one of them put it to me afterwards, my being there made it a concert.

LISTENING TO SLEEP

Now I lay me down to. Where did I hear that? A way of taking leave for the night, let the waking world spin on beyond us, until we surface again. A humble prayer that we will return, that our place will still be there.

The listening mind races ahead to complete the phrase. Of sleep, we would rather not have to think about it, that we just let go. And yet, as we lie stretched out on the launching pad, eyes shut tight, we cannot help wander in thought, our ears like sentinels at the edge of the known world.

Beside us in the dark someone is breathing, our partner sharing the bed is breathing so calmly, already gone. We listen to our own lengthening breaths, but sleep doesn't come. Hitch a ride next door? Almost. Before we know it, before we know.

Last night late and jetlagged I lay down. Though I couldn't see her nor even hear her breath, I knew she was beside me in the bed; peeked one eye open to make sure. I wasn't falling asleep right away. Why wasn't I falling asleep. Soon, her breathing grew audible. I listened a while to her quiet breathing. Listened to her every breath.

JASON WEISS was born and raised at the Jersey shore, schooled in Berkeley, spent a decade in Paris, and has been living in Brooklyn for 30+ years, working as a writer, editor, and translator. His first book was *Writing at Risk: Interviews in Paris with Uncommon Writers* (1991), followed by books on Brion Gysin, Steve Lacy, Latin American writers in Paris, and the ESP-Disk' record label. He also published *Cloud Therapy* (2015), short nonfiction texts on swimming, and translated books by Luisa Futoransky, Marcel Cohen, and Silvina Ocampo. With Iris Cushing, he co-edited a big book of selected poems by the late California poet Mary Norbert Korte (1934-2022), *Jumping into the American River* (2023).